DR. SAMUEL A. MUDD
and the
Lincoln Assassination

Samuel Alexander Mudd
December 20, 1833 – January 10, 1883

Dr. Samuel A. Mudd
and the
Lincoln Assassination

John E. McHale, Jr.

HERITAGE BOOKS
2007

HERITAGE BOOKS

AN IMPRINT OF HERITAGE BOOKS, INC.

Books, CDs, and more—Worldwide

For our listing of thousands of titles see our website
at
www.HeritageBooks.com

Published 2007 by
HERITAGE BOOKS, INC.
Publishing Division
65 East Main Street
Westminster, Maryland 21157-5026

ACKNOWLEDGEMENTS
Special thanks to Dr. Richard D. Mudd, Michael Kauffman, and John C.
Brennan for their guidance and advice; to my wife, Mary, for reviewing the
manuscript; to Deborah Biber for seeing the book through to completion;
and to Elaine Seidman for suggesting it.

PHOTO CREDITS
Cover: Dr. R. D. Mudd
Courtesy of CBS-TV: 134. By permission of Michael E. Kauffman: 28. Library of
Congress: 12, 19, 51, 54, 113. John E. McHale: 16, 24, 32, 46, 58, 74, 130, 132.
Michael J. McHale: 71. Dr. R. D. Mudd: 6, 14, 52. Sheila M. Mudd: 75.
The National Park Service: 23, 25, 44. Ortelius Design: 38.

International Standard Book Number: 978-0-7884-1691-0

Contents

Chapter / One

Mudd's Double Trouble

For a man who would one day be convicted of murder, Samuel Alexander Mudd started life off quietly enough.

He was born December 20, 1833, on the family plantation in Charles County, Maryland, to Henry Lowe Mudd and his wife, Sarah Ann Reeves. A distant relative of Abraham Lincoln, whose favorite aunt was named Mary Mudd, Sam seemed to have a prosperous future ahead of him—much more so, in fact, than that facing the 24-year-old frontiersman.

While Abe had been brought up in a rustic log cabin and his father had been saved from an

Indian raid by Mordecai Lincoln, Mary Mudd's husband, the Charles County Mudds were landed gentry. They could claim kinfolk among the original Maryland settlers who had arrived on the *Ark* and the *Dove* some 200 years before. Furthermore, "Oak Hill," their estate located nearly 30 miles southeast of the present District of Columbia, had come to them directly on a grant from the renowned Lord Baltimore.

Most of this ancestry, however, held little interest for a growing boy. Farm life in the 1830s was pretty much the same everywhere, especially without modern-day equipment, and Sam Mudd inherited the usual chores. These tasks along with a private school system, were shared with his eight brothers and sisters. Throughout the long winter months, the north wing of the Mudd house was turned into a classroom as well as a chapel where Mass could be held on Sundays. There Sam received most of his education until he was old enough to go away to Frederick, Maryland, at the age of 15. It was also there that he learned to play the piano, flute, and violin and acquired the basic skills that would later enable him to become fluent in three languages.

For fun, when work and school didn't interfere, Sam engaged in various Tom Sawyer-type games—swimming and fishing in old Mill Creek, hunting in the dark forests of nearby Zekiah Swamp, and taking weekend trips with his father into Bryantown or sometimes even Washington.

Still a small city then, Washington was not the national shrine we know today. Beside the gaslights and dusty or cobblestoned streets a visitor would expect to find in any nineteenth-century townsite, there were some other noticeable differences. The Washington Monument, for example, was an unfinished stump. The iron dome and the Statue of Freedom had not yet been added to the Capitol rotunda. A raw-sewage channel ran through the heart of the government district. And the present site of the State Department was a swamp known as Foggy Bottom.

Even then, however, there were exciting touches of glamour: soldiers galloping past on high-spirited chargers, politicians bustling about with important-looking documents, foreign dignitaries attired in strange clothing, and the tall, ramrod figure seated next to him on the buckboard.

Henry Lowe Mudd may have been a man of the soil, but he was no ordinary farmer. Described by one of his granddaughters as a kind and charitable but strict parent, he possessed an inquiring mind and insisted on his children getting as much education as possible. Like many Mudds, he also had a wry sense of humor. A 300-acre tract of land that had apparently given him headaches was listed on the Charles County tax rolls as "Mudd's Double Trouble." Henry Mudd was highly regarded by everyone in the community, and when he died in 1877, former Governor John G. Downey of California was among those attending the funeral.

Sam respected his father. Even more, he loved plantation life and wanted to carry on the family tradition. But he had still another idea taking root in his mind. After considerable soul-searching he decided to follow in the footsteps of his cousin George D. Mudd and become a doctor as well as a farmer.

The only other thing Sam needed to make life complete was to marry his childhood sweetheart, Sarah Frances Dyer, whom he called Frank because he already had a sister named Sarah Frances. But the blossoming young woman suggested that they exercise a little patience. Neither had yet reached 19, Sam faced several more years of college, and she wanted a small taste of fun before settling down as a housewife. So she told him to go ahead and get his education. When he had finished and set himself up in medical practice, he would find her waiting.

Although Sam wasn't too happy with the delay, he knew that Frank had made up her mind, so he packed his bags and took off in the family buggy for a three-year stay at Georgetown College in Washington. On October 9, 1854, he transferred to the Baltimore Medical College where, less than two years later, he received his long-awaited degree.[1]

It was during Sam's stay in Baltimore that a bit of theatrical history was recorded at the Charles Street Theatre. John Wilkes Booth, one of the younger members of a famous acting family, made his debut in *Richard III* on the evening of August 14, 1855. Barely 17, Wilkes was a young man in a hurry. He wanted fame and fortune and he wanted them quickly. Possibly because he wasn't as talented as his father and brothers, he made up for his shortcomings with spectacular physical feats. Leaping to the stage at crucial moments of a play from trees, rocks, and balconies in the background, he soon became known in the trade as a jumper and was often called "the gymnastic actor."

Even so, Booth's initial performance created no instant sensation, and it is highly unlikely that

---

[1] Baltimore Medical College is now a part of the University of Maryland.

Portrait of actor John Wilkes Booth

the busy medical student took precious time out to watch him. However, in an ironic twist of fate, less than a decade later, John Wilkes Booth almost cost Sam Mudd his life.

Chapter / Two

A Plot to Kidnap the President

In August 1857, the powerful Ohio Life Insurance and Trust Company went out of business and touched off one of the worst depressions ever to hit the United States. Factories closed, banks teetered on the brink of disaster, farmers were unable to pay off their debts, and even the mighty industry of railroad-building ground to a halt. Things got so bad that by October 1857, *Harper's Weekly* looked around the country and proclaimed the time "a gloomy moment in history."

Undeterred by all these dire happenings, Samuel Alexander Mudd and Sarah Frances Dyer were married less than a month later. The

wedding took place November 26, 1857, at Sarah's home, and it was the social event of the year for the two families. People came from miles around to witness the joining of these old Maryland dynasties. The wedding reception was a lively one, with singing, dancing, and an occasional joke or two about Sam's wisdom in switching to medicine just when farm prices had begun to plummet. But even as a farmer, Sam wouldn't have suffered too badly. He and most of his neighbors had invested heavily in tobacco, which had risen to become the South's second-largest crop, right behind cotton.

This is not to say that the newlyweds had no problems. On the contrary, they didn't even have a place to live. While waiting for their own house to be completed, they moved in with Sarah's bachelor brother, Jeremiah. And it was during this period that their first child, Andrew Joseph, was born, followed in 1860 by a daughter named Lillian Augusta.

These early years of Sam's married life also marked an era of progress and turmoil for the country at large. The depression was ending, but much greater upheaval lay ahead.

❖ ❖ ❖

The American Civil War was a long time coming. As far back as 1832, South Carolina had

Sarah Frances Dyer at approximately the time of her marriage to Sam Mudd in 1857

The house belonging to Sam and Sarah Mudd. It is located near Waldorf, Maryland, on property that has been in the Mudd family since 1696.

threatened to secede, or leave the Union, but had backed down when President Andrew Jackson sent a small fleet to Charleston with the promise that he would take charge of the fighting himself if need be.

Over the years, Northerners and Southerners had clashed on many topics, ranging from tariffs[2] to slavery. Abraham Lincoln rode these disputes into national prominence as a politician, arguing that "a house divided against itself cannot stand."

Less poetically inclined, John Wilkes Booth took a different path in his search for immortality. A school dropout trying to catch up with his better-known brothers, Junius and Edwin, he had headed south and was carving a niche for himself

---

[2] Tariffs are taxes on imported goods. Tariffs hurt the South more than the North because the South had few factories of its own.

on the stage in Richmond, Virginia, when violence exploded less than 150 miles away during the evening of October 16, 1859.

Antislavery forces under John Brown swept down on the sleepy little Virginia hamlet of Harpers Ferry, where railroads and rivers met en route to Washington and the federal government had built a vital munitions arsenal. Stopping trains, taking prisoners, and shooting at least three people (including a freed slave), Brown and his men threatened the entire region. Before they could spread out to other areas, however, soldiers were rushed up from Washington and either killed or captured most of the invaders. The seven survivors were set to be tried on October 25.

Meanwhile, tensions continued to mount, with Brown's sympathizers burning barns, stables, crops, and farm equipment in surrounding counties and threatening to move down from Ohio with a force of 1,000 armed men to free those in jail. Units of the Virginia militia were ordered onto active duty to help keep the peace. One of the dandies enlisting in a volunteer organization called the Richmond Grays was John Wilkes Booth, who had to borrow a uniform.

During his brief stay in Charles Town, where Brown was executed on December 2, 1859, Booth

apparently decided that military life was not for him.
But he did discover that there were more exciting
things to do than playing make-believe in theater.

Eleven months later, Abraham Lincoln was
elected to the presidency, and South Carolina
withdrew from the Union, to be followed shortly
thereafter by six other states. Then, on April 12,
1861, open warfare broke out, with the rebels
firing on Fort Sumter in Charleston Harbor.
Almost immediately, four additional states joined
the insurgents in their attempt to create a new
country.[3]

❖ ❖ ❖

One state that did not leave the Union—but
that would have if given the chance—was Sam
Mudd's Maryland. Both Maryland and Virginia
completely ringed the District of Columbia, and if
Maryland had joined the Confederacy, the capital
of the United States would have been cut off from
all contact with the rest of the country.

At first, Maryland's governor refused to even
consider secession. Then later when he changed
his mind, army troops occupied Baltimore and
Annapolis, and the state legislators were warned
that they would be arrested if they voted to go
with the South. Thus Maryland became a border
state, with citizens fighting on both sides of the

---

[3] This brought the grand total to 11, not 13, as one would be led to believe
looking at the Confederate flag; neither Missouri nor Kentucky actually
seceded.

Portrait of President Abraham Lincoln, taken four days before his assassination in April 1865. He and Dr. Mudd were distant relatives.

lines and the people at home suffering arrests for little or no reason. Other indignities included seizure or destruction of property and the suppression of local newspapers.

As a Southerner and a native Marylander, Sam Mudd would have been less than human if he had not resented this treatment, but in 1862 he wrote a letter wherein he said:

> *It is the longing of my heart that the same old Star Spangled Banner should continue to wave over the land of the free and the home of the brave! But alas! We know not in what manner it can be brought about.*

Even so—despite inflationary prices, shortages of goods, and patients who were unable to pay their bills—Mudd continued his life as a doctor and farmer. Along the way, he and Sarah added two more sons, Thomas and Samuel II, in 1862 and 1864. Then, during the latter part of the war, a visitor arrived who would change all of their lives forever.

With the South hopelessly losing the war after more than three years of continuous bloodshed, 26-year-old John Wilkes Booth entered on a mad scheme to save the day by kidnapping Lincoln and spiriting him across the Potomac to Richmond. Here Lincoln would be held in exchange for Southern prisoners of war or some kind of peace treaty favorable to the Confederacy. To accomplish this goal, Booth needed an additional horse, and a mutual friend sent him to Dr. William Queen in Charles County.

After presenting his letter of introduction in either October or November 1864, Booth spent Saturday night at the Queen house and accompanied the doctor and his son-in-law, John C. Thompson, to Sunday Mass at St. Mary's Church in Bryantown. There they met Sam Mudd, who told them that his neighbor, Squire George Gardiner, had a horse for sale. That evening, Booth stayed with the Mudds.

As Mudd later recalled the incident, supper was followed by a general discussion about the theater and the oil business[4] as well as some peculiar questions from his guest regarding local roads, the political sentiments of the people, and illegal trade between the North and the South.

Early Monday morning the two men strolled next door to Squire Gardiner's, where Booth purchased an aging, one-eyed horse, saying that he wouldn't need it very long. While they were gone, however, the actor lost a potential fan. Sarah had found some papers lying on the floor and opened them briefly to see what they contained. After reading several lines, she realized that the packet contained a love letter that had fallen out of Booth's overcoat, indicating that "some poor man's home had been wrecked by the handsome face and wily ways of Booth." Indignantly, she threw the offending letter into the fire.

A month later, Mudd met his new acquaintance again on a Washington street, and they enjoyed—with two companions—a passing visit of no great consequence. The next time they got together, things would be considerably different.

---

[4] Booth had invested a substantial amount of his funds in the oil business.

Chapter / Three

A Long and Bloody Night

The clock in Ford's Theatre showed almost 10:10 P.M. as Booth patted the single-shot Derringer in his pocket, glanced around nervously, and started up the dim, winding set of stairs. It was Good Friday, April 14, 1865, and somewhere in a flag-draped box above him sat President and Mrs. Lincoln, Army Major Henry R. Rathbone, and the major's fiancee, Clara Harris. General Ulysses S. Grant, who also was to have been sitting in the presidential box along with Lincoln, had canceled his theater reservations at the last minute. Outside, the streets were noisy with mobs of soldiers and civilians celebrating the recent great victory.

The presidential box at Ford's Theatre. Lincoln sat in the opening nearest to the lower balcony, or Dress Circle.

Just five days before, Robert E. Lee had surrendered to Grant at Appomattox Court House, which meant that the war would soon be over. Now, for the first time in years, a battle-weary Lincoln felt that he could just sit back and relax.

Down on the stage in front of them, a comedy, *Our American Cousin*, was in progress. But while Lincoln chuckled at the funnier lines, Booth was listening with a more professional ear. As an actor, he knew every detail of the play, and he was waiting for just the right moment. Harry Hawk was alone on stage at the time, building up to a speech about a "sockdologizing old man trap," and Booth knew that the joke was a guaranteed laugh-getter. In fact, he was counting on the uproar of the audience to cover the few quick movements he would soon have to make.

Entering the hallway behind the presidential box, he was both pleased and surprised to find that there was no guard on duty. Next he put his eye to the peephole in the door so that he could tell where Lincoln was sitting.

Dr. Richard D. Mudd, grandson of Samuel A. Mudd, examines a hole believed to have been drilled by Booth in the door of the presidential box.

The kidnap-and-exchange plot had been discarded with the collapse of the Confederacy. Now, Booth and his followers planned to wipe out the top leaders of the United States Government in one sweeping bloodbath.

At 10:15, Harry Hawk started the prelude to his fateful speech. Pushing open the door of the box, Booth stepped up to Lincoln, shot him behind the left ear, stabbed Major Rathbone in the arm with a knife he had been carrying in his belt, and then leapt over the railing to the stage below. At this point an event occurred that was to bring Dr. Mudd back into the story unexpectedly.

As Booth fell 12 feet to the hard wooden floor of the stage, one of his spurs caught in the Treasury Guards' flag decorating the presidential box. He twisted in mid-air and landed off balance on his left leg, snapping it just above the instep. Nevertheless, Booth managed to limp past an

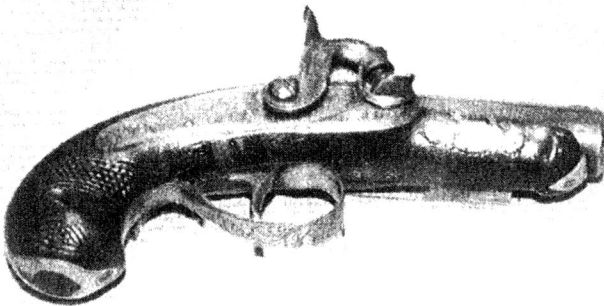

The single-shot Derringer that Booth used to kill Lincoln, now on display at the Ford's Theatre museum

astounded Harry Hawk, shouting Virginia's Latin motto, *Sic semper tyrannis!* ("Thus always to tyrants!"). He vanished backstage and out into an alley where his horse was waiting.

In the bedlam behind him, a doctor probed at the President's gaping wound, stood up sadly, and ordered his dying patient carried across the street to a boardinghouse owned by William Petersen. At 7:22 the next morning, Lincoln died peacefully, stretched across a bed that was much too short for him, and the nation went into mourning. At least part of the nation did. The rest was busy looking for his assassin.

After fleeing the theater, Booth had ridden desperately through the late-evening revelers. He persuaded the guard on the Eleventh Street bridge to let him pass and then forced his tiring horse up the long, steep hill of Anacostia. At the top he paused to wait for David Herold, who had been sent on another assignment and who was now racing to catch up. When Herold finally arrived, he gave a quick report and Booth nodded briskly. The slaughter was well under way.

From here on, time was of the essence, and the men still had a long way to go. Spurring their horses over the crest of the rise, the two fugitives headed in the general direction of southern

Maryland and the hoped-for freedom awaiting them across the Potomac in Virginia.

En route, however, Booth's broken leg began to throb painfully, and he knew he could never make it to safety without medical attention. Then he remembered Dr. Mudd, his host from the previous November. Unfortunately, Dr. Mudd's house was several miles off the highway, and the area would soon be swarming with search parties.

Herold wanted to keep riding, but Booth insisted on the detour. Though scared and tired, Herold nudged his horse into motion and followed Booth through the maze of back country roads to a white frame farmhouse where the Mudd family had been asleep for hours.

As a matter of fact, it was four o'clock on Saturday morning when Herold knocked on the front door and Dr. Mudd climbed out of bed to see who was making all the racket. Herold pointed to his companion, who was wearing a false beard and muffler so that Dr. Mudd wouldn't recognize him, and explained that the man had broken his leg in an accident. Would the doctor be kind enough to look at it? Peering through the darkness, Dr. Mudd agreed, and he and Herold helped Booth into the house. A bed in the second-floor guest room was used for an operating table, and Dr. Mudd slit the actor's riding

The bedroom at the Mudd home, where Booth slept after receiving medical treatment

boot to get to his inflamed, swollen ankle.

Dr. Mudd later told Army investigators that the break had not been a bad one but that he had put a splint on it, bade the strangers goodnight, and proceeded to get some sleep before starting out on his weekend medical rounds.

During the course of these rounds, Dr. Mudd rode into the neighboring village of Bryantown, Maryland, sometime after noon on Saturday and found the place in utter turmoil. People stood around in small groups, chatting and gesturing, while bands of soldiers could be seen almost anywhere he looked. Obviously something big had happened, and it wasn't long before Dr. Mudd heard the rumors that the killer or killers might be hiding in their area.

Adding to this fear was the Army's report that one of the gunman's accomplices had been John H. Boyle, a Confederate terrorist known for his ruthlessness in dealing with Northern enemies. Just the previous November, Boyle had threatened to kill Sam's cousin, Dr. George Mudd, for supporting the reelection of President Lincoln, and in March 1865, Boyle had murdered Thomas H. Watkins, a Union officer recuperating at home from wounds received during the siege at Petersburg. Although it was later discovered that Boyle had nothing to do with Lincoln's murder, the rumors served to keep Bryantown in an uproar.

Hearing all of this, what did Dr. Mudd think about the two strangers at his house? Certainly he knew that neither one of them was Boyle. But what if they were friends of Boyle's or were later joined by Boyle in Sam's absence? What if the three men were holding Mrs. Mudd and the children hostage at this very moment? What would Boyle do if he had the slightest suspicion that Sam might tell the authorities about him? All of these were sobering thoughts, and Sam must have pondered them deeply as he hurried home in the gathering twilight.

Also troubling to Sam was the information he had heard that Lincoln had been killed by an actor named Booth. By any chance, could this be his acquaintance John Wilkes Booth? Offhand he didn't think so, because the pictures being displayed by the soldiers didn't look like Booth. (What no one realized at the time was that the search party had picked up some photographs of Booth's brother Edwin by mistake, and these were the photos being shown around Bryantown.)

Arriving home just as the strangers departed, Sam found Sarah in a state of great concern. The man with the broken leg, she said, had been wearing a false beard, and as he had hobbled down the stairs, it had become partially dislodged. Sam listened to her information in grim silence and then told her what he had heard in Bryantown. Sarah looked shocked as they realized who their visitors had been. Sam said he had better get back to Bryantown and warn someone.

Sarah pleaded with him not to go. The men had just left. If they came back unexpectedly and found her alone, there was no telling what might happen. Sam thought about it. Admittedly, Sarah could be indulging in a little female exaggeration, but the possibility of their return lingered in his mind. Besides, he knew what route the killers had taken because he had told them that morning how to get across Zekiah Swamp. He figured they couldn't get too far with Booth's broken leg. There would be plenty of time to alert the authorities when he took his family to Easter services the next day.

After Sunday Mass, Sam encountered his cousin George and told him about the mysterious doings of Saturday. At Sam's request, George agreed to pass this information along to the soldiers, which he testified he did on Monday, although no action was taken by the Army until Tuesday.

On April 18, 1865—four days after President Lincoln's assassination—Lieutenant Alexander Lovett rode up to the Mudd house at the head of a search party that had tracked Booth all the way from Washington. Lovett dismounted and introduced himself to a slender, balding, reddish-haired man in farm clothing. Although Dr. Mudd was barely 31 years old at the time, his grave appearance and receding hairline made him look considerably older.

Lovett listened noncommittally to Dr. Mudd's story, pausing now and then to ask a few pertinent questions. When did the doctor first hear about Lincoln's death? Did he recognize either of the two strangers? What did they talk about during their visit? How were they dressed? What kind of horses were they riding? Did they say where they had been or, more importantly, where they were going?

Dr. Mudd answered each question as best he could and then led the search party to the edge of Zekiah Swamp. He showed Lieutenant Lovett the same path he had pointed out to the younger of the two fugitives but added that he had not actually seen them go in. Lovett thanked Mudd for his help and waved his hand over his head to signal the rest of the patrol. Six times the men plowed back and forth through the morass, tracing hoofprints, branching out to cover side trails, and constantly looking for clues or something to indicate that Booth had indeed passed this way.

They found nothing. But, thanks to Dr. Mudd, they had picked up two valuable pieces of information: they knew which direction the men

A view of Dr. Mudd's farm, showing the path that Booth and his companion David Herold reportedly took en route to Zekiah Swamp

had taken and, for the first time, they knew that one of them had a broken leg.

On Friday, April 21, the soldiers were back at Dr. Mudd's house to conduct a search. Sam was dining with his father's family and Sarah had to send a servant to fetch him. When Sam returned, he was very cooperative. Neither he nor Sarah had anything to hide. On the contrary, Sam had something of interest to show them that Sarah had found since the soldiers' visit. It was the riding boot he had cut off the bearded man's swollen ankle.

Lieutenant Lovett squinted and peeled back the sliced leather. Inside was some writing. It said: "Henry Lutz, maker, 445 Broadway, New York, J. Wilkes." With this piece of evidence, there could no longer be any doubt about the identity of the two nighttime callers.

Lovett's questions then became more formal. The polite manner and friendly smile were gone. Finally, with the glint of Army steel in his voice, he "invited" Dr. Mudd to accompany him to Bryantown for more interrogation. The questioning continued through Saturday and possibly Sunday. Then, on Monday, came the dread announcement. Sam Mudd was being arrested for participating in the murder of Abraham Lincoln.

Chapter / Four

Death in the Barn

What had become of John Wilkes Booth? Shortly after leaving Dr. Mudd's house on April 15, Booth and Herold disappeared into Zekiah Swamp with their horses. Despite all the search parties and mounted patrols in the area, neither of the men was spotted again until late that night or early the next morning when they showed up at the home of Samuel Cox, about seven miles beyond Bryantown. Of the two people who claimed to have witnessed their arrival, one said that the killers enjoyed a lengthy visit that night with Cox while the other reported that they did not. But no one denied that the two men stayed on Cox's property until Thursday, April 20.

A middle-aged planter, whose son had fought in the Confederate army, Cox not only risked his own life in hiding Booth and Herold but also scorned the $100,000 reward that had been posted for their capture. Instead, he let them hide in a thicket on his grounds and sent one of his relatives, Thomas A. Jones, to bring them food, brandy, and newspapers every day. Jones also periodically scouted around and told them what the Army was up to.

Booth appreciated the help that Cox and Jones had given him but was eager to get moving again. To begin with, several of Cox's former slaves had seen Booth ride up, and Booth wasn't too sure how well they could be trusted. Besides, there was always the chance that some cavalry patrol might blunder into his hiding place by sheer luck. So they had Jones shoot the two horses everyone was looking for and had him scout out a safe path to the Potomac River.

On the night of April 20, 1865—six days after he had brought the whole country out in pursuit—Booth climbed up on a borrowed horse and followed Jones and Herold down to an inlet where a small boat was concealed. Booth was shivering with cold and asked for a cup of coffee, but Jones said it was too dangerous to light a fire. Instead he offered them some meat and bread. The men ate a hasty supper and then, about 300 yards from shore, started a steep descent to the water.

It was a difficult journey, but soon the three men were in a 12-foot flat-bottomed boat, rowing out into the powerful current of the Potomac. Suddenly the men froze. Looming in the middle of the stream ahead of them was a Navy patrol vessel. The two crews spotted each other at about the same time. Shots rang out, men shouted, and searchlights swept back and forth across the water. Frantically, Booth, Jones, and Herold paddled for shore and hid in the marshes while the landing party probed noisily through the underbrush.

Thanks to Jones's knowledge of the area, no one found the three men. The next night Booth and Herold rowed upstream alone and hid for still another day before darting across the Potomac on Saturday night, April 22, to the supposed haven of Virginia. But safety was still a long way off. Behind them, the hunt was getting hotter. As Booth had feared, a former slave had led detectives to the inlet where the boat had been stored, and before long, pursuit had spread to the southern shore.

After resting Sunday morning, Booth and Herold contacted a friend of Jones's, who eventually put them in touch with a guide who owned a horse that Booth could ride. That evening the three men reached the home of Dr. Richard Stuart, only to be told that the doctor was not a surgeon and didn't have room to put them up overnight. But Stuart did lead them into his kitchen and provided a cold snack. Back on the road and growing wearier by the minute, Booth and Herold finally found lodging in the shanty of a free Black named William Lucas. Satisfied that he had done his job, their guide left them and returned home.

In the morning, Lucas hitched up a team and drove the fugitives inland to Port Conway, where they could catch a ferry across the Rappahannock River to Port Royal. While waiting for the ferry, they met three former Confederate soldiers, and either Booth or Herold whispered who they were to the soldiers. Impressed, the soldiers led the fugitives that afternoon to the farm of a man named Richard Garrett, telling Garrett that Booth was a wounded war veteran and that they would be back for him the following day.

As the events developed, however, the end of the trail had been reached. Union forces, who had apparently been tipped off, trapped one of the three Confederates in Bowling Green, Virginia, and to save his own hide, he told them where

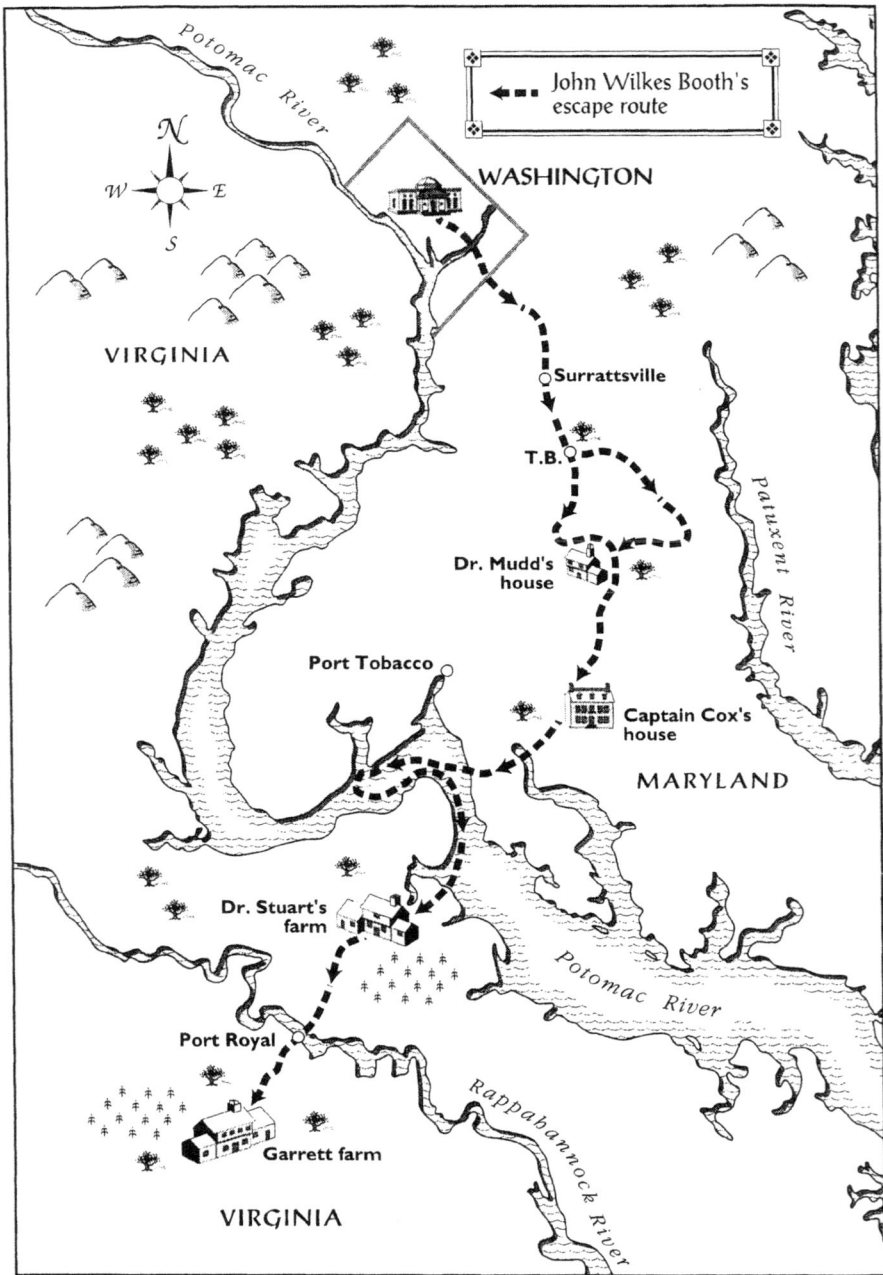

The dashed line shows John Wilkes Booth's escape route following his assassination of President Lincoln on April 14, 1865. Historians are not certain which road was taken between the town of T.B., Maryland, and Dr. Mudd's house.

Booth and Herold were concealed. Lincoln's killer now had less than 12 hours to live.

Shortly after midnight on April 26, the drum of hooves came pounding up to the Garrett farm as a mounted patrol swung in through the gate and demanded entry into the house. But Booth wasn't there. He and Herold had been hidden in a tobacco barn. Quickly the soldiers surrounded the barn and ordered the two men to come out. Booth pleaded for time and was given five minutes. When the threat was made to burn down the barn, Herold surrendered, but still Booth refused to budge.

The threat became a reality as the barn was set on fire. While flames leapt through the hay and timbers, Booth could be seen hobbling and shouting inside. Finally a shot rang out as Sergeant Boston Corbett fired through a crack in the barn, and the actor fell mortally wounded. Two officers dashed in and dragged Booth outside. There he was laid under a tree or on the Garrett porch, depending on the witness telling the story.

But Booth was too far gone to even take a sip of water. As the sky began to lighten with the dawn, he gasped hoarsely, "Tell mother I died for my country." Several minutes later he breathed his last.

Chapter / Five

A Nightmare Come True

When invading British troops burned the nation's Capitol on August 24, 1814, Congress found itself without a home for five years. During most of that time, legislative sessions were held in a private building across the street, on the corner where the Supreme Court now stands. It was outside these temporary quarters that President James Monroe took his oath of office in 1817, and it was inside the same aging structure—then known as Hill's Boarding House—that senator and former Vice President John C. Calhoun spent the last few months of his life, in 1850.

At the start of the Civil War, the dingy old red-brick edifice entered still a third phase of its

colorful existence when the government converted it into a jail, called the Old Capitol Prison.
The windows overlooking the broad Capitol lawn
were now barred tight. The walls, rotted and
infested with vermin, allowed winter winds to
whistle through the many cracks. Rats scampered
across the floors. The jail food was greasy, moldy,
and half-cooked. Rooms were jammed to over-
flowing, and dirt covered everything. The warden,
William P. Wood, was described as stern at best
and tyrannical at worst. All in all, as one visitor
put it, "A gloomier, more terrible-looking prison
did not exist in the land." Bleak and grim as it
was, this was where the soldiers deposited Dr.
Mudd on April 24, following his arrest and interrogation in Maryland.

Technically, Dr. Mudd was placed in a
wooden annex known as Carroll Prison, rather
than in the Old Capitol Prison itself. But the dis-
tinction made little difference to those confined
there. When the original jail had begun to bulge
with 2,000 Confederate soldiers, a block of nearby
homes had been taken over, consolidated, and
given the name of a neighboring street. Soon it,
too, was crowded, and the living conditions
became just as intolerable. Even so, the doctor
remained cheerful and wrote Sarah a letter at the

end of the week. Dated April 29, 1865, it read:

> *I am well. Hope you and the children are
> enjoying a like blessing. Try and get some
> one to plant our crop. It is very uncertain
> what time I shall be released from here. Hire
> hands at the prices they demand. Urge them
> on all you can and make them work.*
>
> *I am truly in hopes my stay here will be
> short, when I can return again to your fond
> embrace and our little children.*

What Dr. Mudd didn't know was that he had
been caught up in a gigantic dragnet sweeping
through the countryside with a vengeance.
Among those arrested were several others from
southern Maryland; the Virginia doctor who had
given Booth a free meal; the livery stable operator
who had rented Booth his horse; a Portuguese sea
captain; and the owner of Ford's Theatre, even
though he had been a hundred miles away the
night of Lincoln's assassination.

Much more ominous was a group of prisoners
too special to be kept in either Carroll or the Old
Capitol. They had been placed aboard two Union
warships anchored out in what is now the
Anacostia River. Soon Dr. Mudd and a woman prisoner in the Old Capitol would be joining them.

Like his original plan to kidnap the President and carry him south, Booth's subsequent murder plot was anything but a lone-wolf operation. One conspirator had been assigned to hold the actor's horse. Two more had been scheduled to kill the Secretary of State. Another had been slated to shoot or stab the Vice President and two others— left over from the failed abduction of the President—had been included for good measure. Still another one was the owner of the house where most of the scheming had taken place.

By April 24, six members of the ring had already been taken into custody. How long the prisoners were kept aboard the ships is not certain, but prior to their first courtroom appearance, they were smuggled ashore in the dead of night to cells in the old Arsenal building. Located on a peninsula known as Greenleaf's Point, the Arsenal commanded an impressive view of the river. Part of the original structure is still standing on the grounds of what is now Fort McNair, home of the National War College.

The view, however, was wasted on the eight miserable prisoners. In addition to being thrown into a series of damp, narrow warrens, all except the woman were shackled and hooded. The last was an especially vicious torture, because the

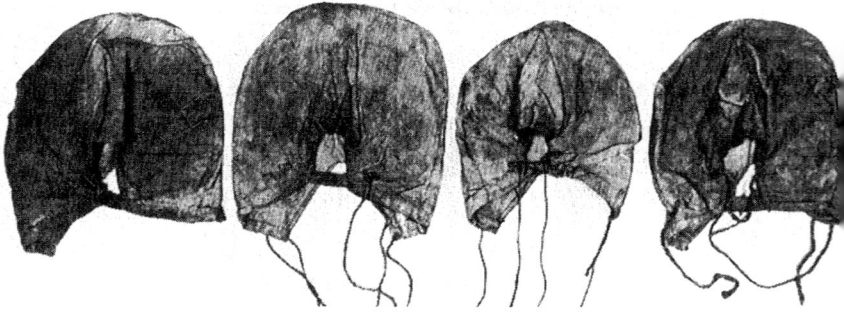

Shown above are the padded hoods, wrist shackles, and leg chains worn by the Lincoln assassination defendants.

canvas bags placed over the men's heads had no eye openings and only tiny slits for the nose and mouth, through which the wearers had to feed themselves. Inside, the cotton padding pressed against the eyes and ears, and during the hot summer days, the faces under the hoods began to swell and itch unbearably. Eventually one of the men went insane from the brutal restriction.

Then, on the morning of May 9, the hoods were taken off and the prisoners were led stumbling, blinking, and scratching in the bright light, into a courtroom on the top floor of the Arsenal. For his part, Dr. Mudd tried to exude some air of composure as he took his seat, but it wasn't easy when he felt so dirty, sweaty, and disheveled. Psychologically he was also benumbed by the realization that what he had kept telling himself couldn't *possibly* happen *had* happened. That he and this bunch of ruffians he didn't even know had been charged with conspiring to murder the President of the United States was his worst nightmare come true!

As the freshly painted room began to throb with the growing crowd of senior military officers and high-ranking civilians—not to mention guards, judges, and members of the press—Sam Mudd let his eyes run down the line of chairs beside him. What he saw was not too encouraging.

Residential quarters at Fort McNair, Washington, D.C. This is all that remains of the building where Dr. Mudd stood trial in 1865. Four of his fellow defendants were hanged on the grounds outside.

- *Lewis Powell,* alias Lewis Payne, a handsome 20-year-old giant with coarse black hair, broad forehead, and muscular chest, who had been wounded while fighting for the South at Gettysburg. As stupid as he was big, Powell had been given an important role on the night of the assassination. While Booth was sneaking up the theater stairs in the dark, Powell had bluffed his way into the home of Secretary of State William H. Seward and tried to stab the cabinet member to death. Fortunately, Seward had been wearing a brace from a recent accident, and the knife had failed to strike a fatal blow. Now Powell stared vacantly into space as his low mentality drifted into madness from more than a week of wearing the canvas hood. Later during the course of the trial, Sam would discover that Powell had been riding the one-eyed horse that Booth had purchased from Sam's neighbor six months before.

- *David Herold*, a 23-year-old pharmacist's clerk with a stooped figure and the immaturity of a boy ten years younger. In addition to having deserted Booth in the Garrett barn when the soldiers threatened to burn it down, Herold had ridden off and left Powell in the Seward house after a servant had run outside calling for help.

- *George A. Atzerodt*, a 33-year-old carriage maker and blockade runner who was known as "Port Tobacco" in honor of his hometown on the lower Potomac. Possessed of a thin, receding chin, a sickly complexion, and a consumptive cough, Atzerodt was described by a witness at the trial as having a "generally villainous countenance." Luckily, he also had a weakness for liquor. Sent to kill Vice President Andrew Johnson while Booth was dispatching Lincoln and Powell was attacking Seward, Atzerodt had gone off and gotten drunk instead. Except for this, Seward's brace, and Grant's change of plans, the United States Government might well have lost four of its top leaders that night.

- *Edman (Ned) Spangler*,[5] a 40-year-old stagehand at Ford's Theatre who was supposed to have held Booth's horse during the assassination but who had been too busy and had turned that chore over to one of his assistants.[6] Sandy-haired and nervous, Spangler had gotten his start in life as a carpenter on the Booth estate in Bel Air, Maryland. On April 14, however, his old ties had gotten him into trouble. As Booth limped past the footlights and shouted his challenge to the world, Spangler temporarily blocked the pursuit backstage and struck at one of the men who was chasing Booth.
- *Samuel Arnold*, a 28-year-old former Confederate soldier who had gone to school with Booth. After participating in two unsuccessful kidnap attempts in January and March—when Lincoln had failed to show at the appointed place—Arnold washed his hands of the whole affair and left town. The fact that he had been in Baltimore at the time of the assassination and knew nothing about it wasn't enough to keep him from being tried along with the others.
- *Michael O'Laughlin*, a 27-year-old former Confederate soldier and boyhood friend of Booth's. Like Arnold, he had been in on the kidnap plot but had drawn the line at murder.

---

[5] Although his true name was Edman, the trial records list it as Edward.
[6] Joseph "Peanuts" Burroughs, the stagedoor guard

And like Atzerodt, he had been on a drinking spree at various Washington bars the night of the shooting. Now he was fighting for his life.

* Mrs. Mary E. Surratt, a 45-year-old widow with a plain face and a stout figure. Mrs. Surratt was the mother of John Surratt—a Confederate agent from Maryland who had participated in the kidnap attempts but not the assassination—and was also the owner of the boardinghouse where the plotters had met. Equally incriminating was the allegation made by one of her employees that she had concealed weapons and other items for Booth on his getaway route through Maryland.

Of the eight defendants, only Sam Mudd—and possibly Mrs. Surratt—could claim innocence of any wrongdoing. Yet one of these two would be hanged before it was all over. Everyone else was obviously guilty of something or other, and Mudd had a sinking feeling as he glanced at the harsh faces of the military judges staring across the bench at him. The country was out for blood, and the court members knew that millions of angry citizens expected them to execute as severe a form of justice as they could.

To accomplish this goal, the government resorted to a little legal chicanery, figuring that the public either didn't know what was going on or wouldn't care. First, the deck was stacked against the hapless civilians by bringing them to trial before a military tribunal, which the Supreme Court ruled a year later as being blatantly unconstitutional. In the meantime the prosecutor blazed still another new trail when he announced that he would try the case under "the common law of war," despite the observation of a former attorney general[7] that there wasn't any such law.

Sitting on the court were seven generals and two colonels, headed by Major Generals David Hunter and Lew Wallace. Although Hunter's record as a battlefield commander had been less than spectacular—permitting the only Confederate invasion of Washington during the entire war—he had been a longtime friend of Lincoln's, and it was expected that he would deal harshly with the band of conspirators gathered before him.

Wallace, on the other hand, had a good military record but would later become much more famous for writing the novel *Ben Hur* while supervising the hunt for a New Mexico gunman known as Billy the Kid. Unlike some other members of the court, Wallace showed no animosity toward Sam Mudd and reportedly made the statement, "If Booth had not broken his leg, we would never

---

[7] Edward Bates, U.S. attorney general, 1861-1864

The members of the court and the prosecutors who convicted Dr. Mudd and sentenced him to life in prison.
Standing (left to right) are Brigadier General T. M. Harris, Major General Lew Wallace, Major General August V. Kautz, and Colonel H. L. Burnett. Judge Advocate General Joseph Holt is seated far right.

have heard the name of Dr. Mudd."

The government's chief counsel in the case was Joseph Holt, judge advocate general of the United States Army. Strongly opposed to slavery, secession, and the Confederacy, Holt had served as Postmaster General and Secretary of War but had recently turned down the job of Attorney General. He was a tough prosecutor and took pride in that reputation. There was no doubt that he would push for a conviction with everything in him.

On the opening day of the trial, the defendants were finally given a chance to hire lawyers, and Sam Mudd, Ned Spangler, and Sam Arnold were lucky enough to latch on to Thomas Ewing, Jr., a 35-year-old general in the Union army. Son of a former senator and, himself, a former chief justice of the Kansas Supreme Court, Ewing also could lay claim to being the brother-in-law of one of the

A sketch of Sam Mudd, drawn during his trial by one of the judges, Major General Lew Wallace, who later wrote the classic novel, Ben Hur

North's top war heroes, General William T. Sherman. In a military court, these were extremely good credentials to bring to the bar of justice.

Mrs. Surratt hired Reverdy Johnson, a former senator from the state of Maryland and former U.S. attorney general. She was not quite as fortunate in her choice. The rest of the defendants picked an assortment of lesser-known attorneys and entered pleas of "not guilty" to charges of either conspiring to kill the President or of aiding Booth and Herold in their attempt to escape.

On May 12, 1865, the first witness was called. The trial of the century was about to begin.

Chapter / Six

The Trial of the Century

Altogether, nearly 350 witnesses testified during a span of six weeks, bringing up such unrelated topics as Confederate plans to wreck Northern waterworks, sink Mississippi riverboats, burn New York City, and start smallpox epidemics in the Union army.

As a result of this hodgepodge, it was May 16 before the government got around to calling its first witness against Dr. Mudd. The doctor refused to panic or break under the pressure. Despite the jails, the hoods, the ships, the chains, and the other mistreatment he had undergone since his arrest three weeks before, he still seemed to

A woodcut depicting the Lincoln assassination courtroom. The prisoners are located at the far end of the room.

believe that justice would prevail and that everything would soon be straightened out. According to one of the reporters at the trial, Mudd just sat there with his mild blue eyes, a hopeful temperament, and the confident air of a man who felt sure he'd be released when the judges discovered what a terrible mistake had been made. Before long, however, that confident air began to disintegrate under the attacks of the prosecution.

Starting with Lieutenant Lovett, several people told the story of Booth's visit to have his broken leg tended, of his hasty flight through Zekiah Swamp, and of the search party's extensive investigations at the Mudd house. Taken at face value, the testimony was neither good nor bad, but the impressions left with the court were obviously aimed at making Dr. Mudd *appear* to be guilty.

At least two witnesses, for example, hinted that he had not been as cooperative with the authorities as he might have been. They indicated that he had been deliberately hiding the telltale boot and had produced it only when he thought the soldiers were getting ready to search his house. (Oddly enough, no one pointed out that it would have been much easier for him to have simply burned the boot or to have sunk it somewhere in the nearby swamp if he hadn't been saving it to show them.)

There were also intimations that Mudd had deliberately delayed reporting Booth's visit to give the killer a head start in his flight south, and that he had pretended not to recognize the fugitive's photograph.[8]

As late spring changed into early summer, Dr. Mudd sat quietly in his chair with his shirtsleeves rolled up and a damp white cloth knotted around his neck. By now the courtroom had become quite familiar to him. Stretching out 30 feet in length and 25 feet in width, the room was filled with

---

[8] As pointed out in Chapter Three, the picture displayed to him had been that of Edwin Booth, rather than that of John Wilkes Booth.

tables and people. One green-covered table served
the judges while another table accommodated the
prosecutors and defense counsel. A railed-off
section confined the prisoners. The remainder of
the space was given over to reporters and specta-
tors. Consequently the steamy breezes filtering
through the barred windows brought little relief
from the stale air inside the room. There was no
means of spreading even a little bit of air around.

But the weather wasn't the only thing heating
up. As the government built its case of gossip,
rumor, speculation, and innuendo—spiced with
some good old-fashioned table pounding and argu-
ments between the lawyers—the defendants knew
that their lives were on the line.

During the course of the trial, nearly two
dozen witnesses testified against Dr. Mudd, but few
could have been considered really damaging. To
come up with a conviction, the prosecutors had
only two alternatives open to them:

1. They had to establish that Mudd knew who
   Booth and Herold were when they came to
   his house and that he knew what they had
   done (thereby proving that he had been guilty
   of harboring fugitives and of being an accessory after the fact), or

2. They had to demonstrate beyond a reasonable doubt that Mudd had been a part of the conspiracy itself and had actually known in advance of the plot to kill the President.

From a legal standpoint, the first of these goals was totally *impossible* to prove. After all, only four persons in the entire world could testify as to whether Mudd had recognized his visitors and was aware of their actions the night before. Of these four, Booth was dead, Herold wasn't allowed to testify, and Dr. and Mrs. Mudd swore to their dying days that they hadn't realized the man with the beard and muffler had been the actor Dr. Mudd had met only twice in his life and Mrs. Mudd only once. Herold, needless to say, was a total stranger to both Dr. and Mrs. Mudd.

Regarding the second alternative, the government's case boiled down to the sworn testimony of four men. The first, and potentially the most critical, statement was provided by Louis Weichmann, or Wiechmann,[9] one of Mrs. Surratt's boarders. Matter of factly the government clerk told how he had met Dr. Mudd and Booth several months before, while he and John Surratt had been walking down Seventh Street in Washington. He said that the four of them had then gone to Booth's

---

[9] He spelled his name both ways from time to time.

Mary Surratt's former boardinghouse at 604 H Street, where the conspirators held a number of their secret meetings

room in the National Hotel for drinks and cigars. At one point, he testified, the other three had stepped out into the hallway briefly for a private conversation, during which Booth appeared to be scribbling a map or something on the back of an envelope. By way of explanation, Dr. Mudd later told Weichmann that Booth was interested in buying a piece of property and had asked the two Marylanders for their advice. When asked by defense counsel if anything had been done or said in the hotel room to indicate that Booth, Surratt, and Dr. Mudd had been involved in a conspiracy of some kind, Weichmann replied, "No, sir."

Further questioned as to how he was able to date the meeting in mid-January, the government's key witness said that Congress had returned from its Christmas vacation at the time, and he had recently received a letter dated January 6, so he knew that the incident had occurred sometime around the middle of the month. Interestingly, after a hotel clerk proved that the meeting had actually taken place on December 23, 1864, Weichmann noted in his autobiography that he remembered the December date very well because he and Surratt had been out Christmas shopping and he had been impressed with the gaily decorated windows in the local stores.

Two years later, James J. Gifford, who had shared an adjoining cell in Carroll Prison with Weichmann, testified that he had seen a government officer approach his fellow prisoner in 1865 and tell him that if he didn't cooperate with the prosecution, he would be hanged along with the other defendants. Even so—discounting the erroneous dates and the alleged coercion—if all of Weichmann's evidence is taken at face value, he never said one incriminating word against Dr. Mudd.

The second major government witness was

William A. Evans, who claimed that he had a
secret but unpaid commission to arrest "deserters
and disloyalists." He said that the previous winter
he had seen Dr. Mudd entering the Surratt House
on H Street, "a nest of spies," and that the visitor
had been greeted at the door by Mrs. Surratt's
daughter just as one Judson Jarboe was leaving. In
rebuttal, Anna Surratt was put on the stand, and
although she readily admitted having seen the
major conspirators—Booth, Powell, and
Atzerodt—in the boardinghouse, she swore that
she had never seen either Dr. Mudd or Jarboe there.

For his part, Jarboe stated he had never been
to the Surratt house and had never encountered
Dr. Mudd even once prior to the trial.
Furthermore, two of Mrs. Surratt's boarders,
including Weichmann, added that they had never
observed Dr. Mudd on the premises.

By way of explaining his flagrantly perjured testimony, Evans said that, for the past month, he "had
been on the verge of insanity," to which General
Ewing replied, "There is nothing I can add to that."

The third witness in order of importance was
a New York attorney named Marcus Norton.
According to Norton, on the morning of March 3,
1865, he had been preparing some court papers in
his room at the National Hotel when a man he

had never seen before appeared at his door, looking for John Wilkes Booth. Norton said that he had told the stranger how to reach Booth's room but had thought no more about it until he saw Dr. Mudd in the courtroom and identified him as the mysterious caller he had viewed for less than a minute some three months before.

Since Norton had been adamant in dating the incident as having occurred on March 3, and because he had court business on that day, his testimony was easy to debunk. In Mudd's defense, General Ewing produced four witnesses, including a patient who had been staying in Dr. Mudd's house for treatment, to prove that the defendant had not been within 30 miles of Washington on March 3 or any other day that week. As to Norton's credibility, two of his neighbors from Troy, New York, including a local judge, testified that they wouldn't believe anything the attorney said, even under oath, and that that was the "general opinion of the people of Troy."

The last buttress of the government's case was Daniel J. Thomas, who told how, in the latter part of March, he and Dr. Mudd had visited a fellow farmer named John Downing and that the three of them had discussed the approaching end of the war. During the course of this conversation, Thomas claimed, Dr. Mudd predicted that the President, the Cabinet, and other unidentified individuals would be killed in approximately six or seven weeks.

Appearing before the military commission, Downing swore that he had been privy to the entire conversation, and that the remarks attributed to Dr. Mudd had never occurred. In support of this, Thomas's brother, a medical doctor, testified that Daniel suffered from "nervous depression" and that, as a result, both his memory and his sense of reason had been affected. Another doctor was even more emphatic. He said that Daniel was a compulsive liar as well as being insane.

On behalf of the defense, General Ewing introduced considerable evidence to prove that no one knew about the assassination in Charles County until Saturday afternoon, that Dr. Mudd's house was miles removed from Booth's escape route, and that Booth would never have made such an unplanned detour except for the pain in his leg. Step by step, he built up a picture of a kindly country doctor awakened in the middle of the night to treat a stranger's broken leg, only to find himself accused of having participated in a murder conspiracy.

Through succeeding witnesses, Ewing further showed how Mudd had gone into Bryantown on his medical errands, learned about the assassination, returned home to discuss the matter with his wife, and wound up asking his cousin George to notify the authorities. Over heavy objections by Holt—who was trying to depict Mudd as a Southern sympathizer responsible for delaying the pursuit of Booth—Ewing brought out the fact that government investigators had waited more than 24 hours before acting on Dr. Mudd's vital message.

Holt fought, argued, and objected. Since he had no real evidence to present, his whole case hinged on raising doubts and suspicions. As a result, he and General Ewing battled at some length over a simple effort to notify the Army about Booth's visit. Holt was determined not to introduce *any* information that might depict Mudd in a good light.

Even so, General Ewing managed to bring in friends, neighbors, relatives, and former slaves to testify that Dr. Mudd was a kind and considerate man who took his oath of loyalty "with respect and reverence," who referred to Lincoln's death as "an atrocious and revolting crime," and who was a "good, peaceable, and quiet citizen." One neighbor even went so far as to state that he did not know "a more loyal man . . . in the state of Maryland."

Scattered maneuvers in Dr. Mudd's case dragged on through June 12, but the only important chore still remaining was General Ewing's final summation to the court. Pointing to the rumpled, long-suffering doctor sitting dispiritedly between Arnold and Spangler, Ewing reminded his listeners that Mudd had neither murdered anyone nor been proven guilty of treason. In addition, he maintained that the doctor had not participated in any plots against the President, didn't even know the latter was dead when Booth arrived at his house, and had made every effort possible to establish contact with the search parties. Moreover, the doctor had saved the notorious boot for their inspection, given them the valuable information that Booth had suffered a broken leg, and had even told them which direction the fugitives had taken in continuing their flight. Most importantly, he reminded the court, no one had traced Booth to Dr. Mudd's house. The only way the search parties had learned of the visit was through information supplied voluntarily by the doctor himself.

❖ ❖ ❖

At approximately noon, July 6, 1865, Major Generals W. S. Hancock and J. F. Hartranft visited the prisoners and announced the findings of the court, as approved by President Johnson. All eight defendants had been declared guilty, with Herold,

Atzerodt, Powell, and Mrs. Surratt condemned to die the following day. Arnold, O'Laughlin, and Dr. Mudd received life terms in prison. Spangler was sentenced to six years of hard labor.

The surprise of these findings was not that a probably innocent boardinghouse keeper had been ordered hanged with three would-be killers, but that *anyone* had come out alive.

Appeals were quickly submitted on Mrs. Surratt's behalf, and Benn Pitman, the official court stenographer for the trial, stated that he was fully convinced of the poor woman's innocence, but it was all in vain. So, too, was a last-minute visit paid to the White House by Mrs. Surratt's daughter, who threw herself on the floor and started sobbing when the doorman refused to let her in to see the President.

Sometime around 1:30 P.M. on the steaming hot afternoon of July 7, planks were knocked out from under the scaffolding in the penitentiary courtyard, and four bodies plummeted to their deaths. Later the corpses were carried back inside the building where they had been tried and were buried under the old east wing, near Booth's grave. The judges congratulated themselves on a job well done and filed out to other assignments. All that remained now was to get rid of the four living prisoners.

Chapter / Seven

"Abandon All Hope..."

Temporarily, while the Army tried to decide what to do with them, life for the surviving prisoners brightened somewhat. Those who asked for Bibles received them. In addition, they were unchained every day and allowed to stroll leisurely around the grounds for as much as two hours. The fresh air and sunshine brought a welcome relief from the dark cells, even though the guards kept a close watch over the four men and refused to let them talk to one another. But the calm fooled no one. Guards and inmates alike knew that events were rapidly preparing to take a turn for the worse.

When the sentences had been handed down

on July 5, Dr. Mudd, Sam Arnold, Edman Spangler, and Michael O'Laughlin found themselves ordered to be confined at hard labor in the penitentiary at Albany, New York. If that sounded unappealing to a group of Southerners—who pictured themselves working outdoors in freezing winds and icy snows—it nevertheless had certain advantages to offer. For one thing, it meant that their families could visit them and that their lawyers could interview them while working on their cases. Unfortunately the Army knew this, too, and was quietly planning a surprise for all concerned.

On the afternoon of July 17, the prisoners were taken before General Hartranft, military governor for the District of Columbia. Here they were informed that their transportation orders had been changed. Instead of going to Albany, they would be headed for Fort Jefferson, Florida, 70 miles off the tip of Key West in the Gulf of Mexico, and they would be leaving that night, without a chance to say goodbye to anyone.

At first, the change might have seemed like an improvement over the chillier climate of the northlands, but an improvement wasn't what the Army had in mind. Like the prison at Alcatraz Island, located in San Francisco Bay, and the French hellhole Devil's Island, off the coast of South America,

Fort Jefferson was set on a tiny dot of land to make escape as difficult as possible. In the case of Dr. Mudd and his three miserable companions, it may also have been intended to make living as difficult as possible. Certainly no one in Washington ever expected to see them again.

Shackled in irons and chained, they were marched out of their cells at midnight, led down to the Potomac waterfront, and taken aboard a small steamer rocking gently at the pier. After a few quick commands, the gangplank was drawn up. Sparks flew from the smokestack and lights flashed on the shore. Lines were cast off. The helmsman gave his wheel a sharp turn. Soon the steamer was nosing out into the chocolate-brown current. Sam Mudd was on his way to prison.

Less than 18 hours later, the steamer arrived off Old Point Comfort, where the James River joins Chesapeake Bay, not far from the scene of the famous naval battle between the *Monitor* and the *Merrimac*. As the steamer hove to, a tugboat drew up alongside and bumped smoothly into position. Signals were made to transfer the human cargo.

Climbing rope ladders from one ship to another while the two vessels are bobbing about in open water is a tricky exercise for even veteran sailors. Here, a group of landlubbers—a doctor, a carpenter, a feed-store clerk, and a commissary worker—were being forced to do it twice, weighted down with heavy chains. First they had to climb from the steamer into the tugboat. Then, after a short ride, they reversed the procedure by pulling themselves up aboard the gunboat *Florida* for the remainder of the voyage to Fort Jefferson. In a last-minute concession, the guards took the manacles off the prisoners' wrists so that they could maneuver the ladders but then reshackled them once they had reached the dock.

Still more afflictions awaited the four men on board the *Florida*. Their cells were in the stifling hold at the bottom of the ship. To reach the cells, the men had to go down a series of steep ladders whose rungs were farther apart than the lengths of chain binding their ankles. As a result, with each step the manacles rubbed up and down painfully, tearing the skin off the prisoners' legs.

Nor was this a passing, one-time torture. Each morning, for several days, the men had to climb topside to get their rations of fat salt pork and hard biscuits, and each evening they had to grope their way back down so that they could sleep in a room stinking with rotten vegetables and ship's supplies. Such a regimen, over an extended period of time, might well have led to a series of major

infections and possibly the loss of a leg or two had
not a little mercy finally prevailed.

When the ship arrived off Hilton Head Island,
South Carolina, the officers invited a number of
guests aboard for an evening of dancing and
dining. Apparently mellowed by the effects of
their party, the hosts decided to let the prisoners
stay on deck for the rest of the trip, which meant
cool breezes for sleeping at night and an end to
the infernal climbing. In yet another act of
charity, the commander ordered all chains
removed during the daylight hours but had them
replaced again at night.

On the sixth day at sea, a shout went up and
everyone rushed forward to stare in awe as massive
stone and brick walls gradually appeared out of the
water, followed by a thin fringe of palm trees and
then a narrow, white, sandy beach. It was Dr.
Mudd's first glimpse of the end of the world: a
giant-sized oven of shimmering, blistering heat,
without hope or amenities.

On both sides of the ship, in the blue-green
water, lay scattered patches of coral reef covered
with sand and scrubby tufts of undergrowth.
Overhead, huge frigate birds with a wingspan of
almost seven feet wheeled through the sky as the
Florida approached, scattering clouds of smaller

birds, mostly sooty terns that had flown in from Africa to lay their eggs. Beneath the surface, beds of sea ferns swayed with the tide and the waves from the passing ship, while the multicolored "rocks" dotting the beaches turned out to be hawksbill, green, and loggerhead turtles.

When the Spanish explorer Juan Ponce de León first visited the Gulf of Mexico in 1513, he named this group of islands *Las Tortugas*, or "The

Aerial view of Fort Jefferson, located in the Gulf of Mexico, approximately 70 miles west of Key West, Florida

Turtles," for the edible turtles found there. The word "Dry" was added to warn future visitors of the lack of fresh water. Located at the tail end of a 200-mile line of land specks called keys,[10] the reefs are named Garden Key, Bush Key, Loggerhead Key, Sand Key, Middle Key, Long Key, and East Key.

By far the most important of the seven is Garden Key, and as the gunboat worked its way through the narrow channels, Sam could see why. Taking up almost the entire island was a gigantic, six-sided structure, rising nearly fifty feet high and stretching half a mile in perimeter. Its walls were a good eight feet thick and boasted three gun tiers designed to house 450 cannons.

Situated in the middle of the strait separating Florida from Cuba, the Dry Tortugas presented an ideal gateway to protect the southern United States coastline, much like Gibraltar guards the entrance to the Mediterranean. Observations to this effect came as early as 1829, but it wasn't until 1846 that work on the fortress finally got under way. Since there were no natural building materials available on site, everything—including stone, bricks, wood, iron, glass, and all the furnishings—had to be ferried over from the mainland. So too did the workers. Because of this, construction progressed slowly and at great expense.

---

[10] From the Spanish word *cayo*, or small island

In fact, much work still needed to be done when the South seceded from the Union in 1861, and the fortress was far from complete at the time of Lincoln's assassination four years later. As for the cannons, most of them never arrived.

Christened Fort Jefferson, the fortress was used primarily during the war years to scare off blockade runners, but two events doomed its future as a military model. Shortly after Dr. Mudd's arrival, Army engineers discovered that the foundations of the heavy walls had not been sunk into hard coral as previously thought, but into a mixture of loose rocks and sand. Furthermore, the invention of more deadly weapons made it impossible for a structure such as Fort Jefferson to survive a concentrated bombardment from modern warships.

Amazingly the sixteen-acre citadel is still standing today, but its only brushes with combat came during the Spanish-American War in 1898, when the battleship *Maine* stopped there before being blown up in Havana Harbor, and during World War I, when the Navy built a coaling station outside the fortress walls. Since then, the islands have been converted into a national park and wildlife preserve.

To the people aboard the *Florida* in 1865, however, Fort Jefferson bore little resemblance to

A view of the moat surrounding Fort Jefferson. Contrary to popular opinion, the moat did not contain sharks.

a park or preserve of any kind. It was grim, forbidding, and surrounded by a moat intended to keep enemies out and prisoners in. Furthermore, the waters encircling the Keys have long been known as an area where sharks and barracuda cruise in search of floating snacks.

Cowed as they were, the four newcomers realized that escape was most unlikely. Later they would hear tales about a number of inmates who had fled at one time or another, but since none of them was ever seen again, it was presumed that they were polished off by the sharks, the storms, or the heat.

As a penitentiary, Fort Jefferson lasted slightly over a decade. Because of poor health conditions, maintenance expenses (even today, drinking water has to be brought in from Key West), staff morale problems, and constant hurricane damage, it was closed down in 1874. More than a century later, vacationers standing in the center of the quiet parade ground often find it difficult to picture the suffering and death that form such an important part of the island's history.

❖ ❖ ❖

As the *Florida* approached Fort Jefferson on July 24, 1865, it touched off a signal shot, and the island garrison fired a round in reply. Shortly thereafter, the duty officer was rowed out to the

One of the inner passageways at Fort Jefferson, leading to Dr. Mudd's cell

gunboat and made arrangements for the prisoners to be taken ashore. There they were placed in a gun casement while the officer in charge of the installation explained the rules and regulations to them. Particularly he warned them that, if they misbehaved, they would be committed to a dark and gloomy dungeon, over the door of which hung a quote from *Paradise Lost:* "Abandon all hope, ye who enter here."

The prisoners were then given wooden planks to sleep on, and they stretched out to get some rest. As Dr. Mudd closed his eyes in despair, all he could think about was escaping and getting back to his family. Instead, he would wind up in the dungeon of horrors that he had been so sternly warned about.

Chapter / Eight

To Flee or Not to Flee

Early the next morning, Dr. Mudd and the three other prisoners got their first good look at the island where everyone assumed they would die. After eating a breakfast of weak coffee and bread—mixed with bugs, sticks, and dirt—they were turned loose to roam both the interior and exterior grounds. According to Sam Arnold, who later wrote a book about his experiences, the sun gleaming on the sand was so bright that it often caused a form of eye damage that made it difficult to see at night. For this reason it was called moon blindness.

On August 24, Dr. Mudd wrote his wife to report that he had been at Dry Tortugas exactly

one month. He announced that he was in reason-
ably good health and had been helping out in the
prison hospital but was suffering greatly from
homesickness. He expressed concern about the
well-being of Sarah and the children and even
feared that the reason he hadn't received any mail
was because someone had died and his friends
were afraid to tell him.

Then, on September 5, he mentioned the one
word that had been eating away at his mind ever
since his arrival: escape. He told Sarah that he
had already rejected several opportunities to slip
away from the island because this might look like
an admission of guilt on his part. Now he was
beginning to change. He said that he had given up
hope of receiving either justice or mercy from the
government and that he sometimes wondered if
he would ever see his loved ones again. He glumly
remarked that, if he could find an honorable way
to leave the United States, he would like to take
his family and move to another country.

Three meals a day, Dr. Mudd lived on coffee,
bread, and butter, padded out a couple of times
with potatoes, onions, and molasses.
Unfortunately, as he noted, vegetables didn't last
long in the oppressive climate, and he labeled the
pork and beef "poisonous."

The work, on the other hand, wasn't too strenuous, and that gave him plenty of time to think. Too much time, perhaps. Watching a transport arrive in early September, he wondered how difficult it would be to hide on such a ship until it reached a mainland port where he could slip ashore in the darkness. Since he was not a physically big man, he realized that the alternative of stealing a small boat and trying to row seventy miles or more was completely out of the question. Nor could he ask anyone else to join him, because they might report him to the guards in hopes of receiving a reward. So he decided that he would have to flee alone.

❖ ❖ ❖

On September 25, 1865, his chance came with the arrival of the transport *Thomas A. Scott*, en route to New York City. Removing his prison uniform and changing into a set of civilian clothes, he boarded the *Scott* with a young crewman named Henry Kelly, who may have been bribed to furnish the clothing and a place to hide. Together the two men strolled along the deck as if on routine business. Then, when no one was looking, they scurried down to the hold of the vessel, where Kelly lifted up a loose plank and Dr. Mudd climbed under it. Later, once the lines had been cast off and people were busy about their chores, Kelly promised to return with something to eat.

Instead, disaster struck. One of the other crewmen had spotted the stowaway accompanying Kelly and had rushed ashore to tell the nearest soldiers. A patrol quickly assembled on deck, spread out around the ship, and began probing into every nook and cranny large enough to conceal a human being.

In his hiding place, Dr. Mudd scarcely dared breathe as the heavy boots drew nearer. He listened to the shouting and noise coming from the passageways above him and the fetid water sloshing in the darkness below him. He felt hot and dizzy, but he clung to a slippery wooden support for dear life. He prayed. He closed his eyes. He imagined what it would be like to see his family again. He thought of what it would be like *not* to see his family again. And then the blade of a sword flashed between the planks and struck Sam in the leg. He had been found!

Triumphantly the soldiers yanked the terrified prisoner from his tiny compartment, twisted his arms behind him, and half-dragged, half-marched him topside to announce the success of their mission. Stumbling off the ship, Sam was taken immediately before Major George E. Wentworth, the angry commanding officer.

Wentworth was more than just angry. He was scared. The whole time the search for his missing ward had been going on, he had paced up and down, imagining what sort of punishment the Army would mete out to him for letting one of the Lincoln conspirators escape in broad daylight—especially after Washington had just warned him that a scheme was afoot to free the four men.

Slightly over a month before, General Lafayette Baker, head of the Secret Service, had notified the War Department that an armed band was gathering in New Orleans to attack Fort Jefferson. The Secretary of War, in turn, had alerted his divisional commanders in the South, and General Phil Sheridan had personally sent a lieutenant to Florida to tell every unit to be on the watch for any suspicious activities.

Eyes flashing with suppressed fury, Major Wentworth jabbed a finger in the direction of Dr. Mudd and Seaman Kelly, ordering them both to be thrown into the dungeon in chains. He then dictated a memorandum to the provost marshal, ordering that Dr. Mudd be relieved of his hospital duties and be sent to the engineering department for "hard labor," pushing sand in a wheelbarrow. Moreover, the major wrote, any time a ship was in harbor, Dr. Mudd was to be chained and thrown into the dungeon until such time as the ship left.

Knowing that he had brought this punishment down upon himself, Sam offered no complaints, but he did regret the suffering he had caused Kelly and the other Lincoln conspirators, who had been thrown into chains along with him.

Kelly's story, however, possibly had a happy ending. Less than a week after being locked up, he and another prisoner freed themselves from their fetters, broke an iron-gated window, and climbed down the wall using the chains with which they had been bound. Then, under cover of darkness, they put out to sea in a small boat loaded with supplies stolen from an island storeroom. Whether they eventually made it to safety is not known.

In recounting this incident, Dr. Mudd told his family that six other prisoners had reportedly made good their escape on the *Thomas A. Scott* the same day he had tried. As fate would have it, the soldiers had discovered Sam first and had been so elated at their good fortune that they never even considered the need to search for anyone else.

When the heavy metal door slammed shut behind Dr. Mudd and his associates, they glanced around the dimly lit cell and discovered that they were not alone. Already scattered about the floor in chains were a group of former Confederate soldiers, including one of the most colorful men to have ever worn the uniform.

Colonel George St. Leger Grenfell had been born May 30, 1808, in London, England. By the time Dr. Mudd stumbled over him in the dark, he was in his late fifties and had long, graying hair and leathery skin. Compared to the young warriors sharing his misery, he appeared to be a battered shell of a man, but looks often prove to be deceiving.

In actuality, Colonel Grenfell was a famous soldier of fortune and, even now, he was busy planning a means of escape. Slowly he rose to his feet and studied the newcomers through a pair of faded-out, watery blue eyes.

Like Dr. Mudd, he stood slightly under six feet, but, unlike Dr. Mudd, he was literally a man of the world. Having run away from home at an early age, he had joined the French Foreign Legion to fight the Riffs and Tuaregs in North Africa, served under Giuseppe Garibaldi in South America, helped put down the Sepoy uprising in India, and joined the British army for the Crimean War against the Russians. More recently he had come to the United States to study the campaigns of the Civil War and had decided to cast his lot with the Confederates.

Commissioned Inspector General under Braxton Bragg, Grenfell served briefly with John Hunt Morgan's raiders before agreeing to take part in a grandiose scheme to split the Union in half and force either Congress or the President to sue for peace. According to the plan, Confederate undercover agents were to break into Northern prison camps in the states of Ohio, Indiana, Illinois, Michigan, and Wisconsin; free the Southern soldiers held captive there; and assist them in destroying or capturing a number of major midwestern cities.

Thanks to Lafayette Baker's spies, though, the Secret Service soon discovered what was going on, and most of the plotters were rounded up before they could carry out their assignments. Colonel Grenfell was among this group. Arrested in Chicago, he stood trial in Cincinnati and was sentenced to be hanged, spared only by his British citizenship. Besieged by a flood of letters from across the Atlantic and by a series of articles in the London newspapers, President Andrew Johnson decided not to rock the international boat. Instead, he canceled the execution and ordered Grenfell moved to Fort Jefferson. There the colonel and Dr. Mudd formed what would prove to be a valuable alliance.

Chapter / Nine

A Lump of Flesh and Blood

The two groups of men lodged in the dungeon had been imprisoned for serious crimes committed against the government. Other than that, they shared very little in common. Some were Westerners and soldiers; some were Easterners and civilians.

Given these discrepancies, things worked out surprisingly well. Everyone appreciated having a doctor on hand, and the discovery that Arnold and O'Laughlin had served in the Confederate army cemented their relations with the other prisoners who were, or had, been soldiers themselves. Friendships gradually began to develop, with the most unlikely one involving Colonel Grenfell, the toast of five continents, and Sam Mudd, the small-town physician and farmer.

A descendant of British colonizers himself, Mudd hungrily devoured the older man's tales of marching through swamps, fighting in deserts, viewing rebel atrocities in India, and riding with Morgan's cavalry through waves of Union horse troops.

To those watching them, it soon became apparent that the men were more alike than different. In particular, both possessed hot tempers and stubborn streaks, which did not endear them to the authorities who ran Fort Jefferson. Each also possessed a strong sense of determination. Mudd's, less daring, had nearly enabled him to escape; Grenfell's almost certainly led to his death.

When the prisoners were finally released from the dungeon, gone were the soft jobs. Instead of working in the hospital and the provost marshal's office, Dr. Mudd and Sam Arnold had been turned loose in the hot sun to scrape and stack bricks for construction on the fort. Glad to be away from the sick rooms, where men were dying regularly from unidentified tropical diseases, Mudd nevertheless refused to play the model prisoner for his guards. As they seethed in frustration, he spent an entire day cleaning one brick.

Grenfell, driven by the same tenacity, went even further. After slaving with a thirty-pound ball chained to his leg, unloading tons of coal, his body began to collapse. He announced that he could do no more. Unmercifully he was informed that if he didn't work, he wouldn't eat. The colonel stared in return but failed to move. As they were at an impasse, the guards resorted to more drastic measures. They tied him to a grate outside the prison walls where the sun could beat down on him all day and the flies and mosquitoes could buzz and bite to their heart's content. Not even that, however, could break the older man's spirit.

Seeing that he was losing this battle of wills, the lieutenant in charge of the work detail ordered Grenfell taken down to a nearby wharf. There, with his chains removed but his hands tied behind him, he was thrown into the Gulf of Mexico. Sputtering and handicapped as he was by the ropes, Grenfell struggled to the surface and managed to keep his head above water by using his legs to tread water. This so infuriated the lieutenant that he ordered soldiers to bind Grenfell's legs and throw him back into the gulf. Still the prisoner succeeded in floating on his back until he was hauled onto the wharf and weights were added to his legs. This time he sank helplessly to the bottom in twenty feet of water and stayed there drowning until the lieutenant had him raised.

"Now will you work?" the officer growled.

Grenfell shook his head.

Three more times he was thrown back into the water until he fainted from the liquid in his lungs. Then the lieutenant kicked him viciously and stalked away from the soggy, inert lump of flesh and blood. Later, a kindly guard sneaked out, untied the colonel, helped revive him, and wrapped a blanket around him as night began to set in.

The next morning's dawn brought the usual activities, ranging from reveille and inspections to flag-raising ceremonies and the posting of duties. When the lieutenant from the guard detail finished his breakfast and headed for the main gate leading out of the prison, he was greeted by an astonishing sight. Standing in front of him was the man he had left for dead the day before. Dirty, wet, unshaven, cut, battered, and bruised, Grenfell snapped sharply to attention.

Blinking at this display, the lieutenant had only one thought in mind. "Going to pick up those bricks now, Grenfell?"

Stubbornly the prisoner shook his head, and passersby paused to see what would happen next.

Like two statues, the men stood there facing each other—toe to toe, eyeball to eyeball—and finally it was the lieutenant who broke. Grunting something under his breath, he stepped around Grenfell and headed off toward the beach.

❖ ❖ ❖

On November 11, 1865, Dr. Mudd wrote a letter to his brother-in-law, Jeremiah Dyer, asking Jere to contact the British ambassador in Washington to see if he could do anything for Grenfell. Obviously impressed with his newfound friend, Mudd described him as intelligent, witty, and fluent in several languages. More importantly, he explained that Grenfell was suffering from wounds and disease, lack of medical treatment, the wearing of heavy chains, and "loathsome food." If something weren't done soon, Mudd warned, Grenfell would be dead in a short time.

Possibly because of this plea—or possibly because Grenfell's relatives in England had contacted the Prime Minister—a letter was sent to the State Department, protesting the "barbaric conditions" then in existence at Fort Jefferson.

The Army denied everything. In a letter written by someone who had probably never been to the Dry Tortugas in his entire life, Garden Key was made out to be a Caribbean resort. The work was light, the weather was pleasant, and Grenfell appeared to be quite happy for a man in jail. Eventually the true story surfaced when the old warrior managed to smuggle out a letter to his daughter, describing the tortures he had undergone.

As Dr. Mudd and his new friend exchanged ideas on how to cope with their life sentences, each began to realize that they had basic differences of philosophy. Grenfell felt that the only solution lay in escape, and the sooner the better. Mudd preferred to wait for a presidential pardon, since he didn't want to spend the rest of his life hiding as a fugitive from justice. Unfortunately, he had to admit, his prospects at the moment didn't seen too promising.

Time was slipping away, and two recurring themes kept running through his letters home: a fear that not enough was being done to obtain his release and concern that he was unable to get to church on Sundays.

As a practicing Catholic, Dr. Mudd worried because he hadn't attended Mass or received communion since arriving at Fort Jefferson. He had a rosary with him and said it every day. He also, as he wrote Sarah, tried to follow the religious training he had received as a youth and hoped that God would some day bring the two of them together again in this life. If not, he wrote, surely they would meet in the next.

Meanwhile, he continued to yearn for the formal celebration of Mass shared with a congregation of fellow Christians. To his delight, his prayers were answered on December 28, when Father James O'Hara arrived by ship from Key West bringing with him Bishop Augustin Verot, of Savannah, Georgia, who also served as Vicar Apostolic for the state of Florida.

There is no indication that Dr. Mudd and the prelate had ever met before, but as a young priest, Bishop Verot had been assigned to a parish in Clarksville, Maryland, where he had worked primarily with poor slaves and rejoiced when they gave him their confidence. Later, during the international meeting of bishops and cardinals known as Vatican Council I, he would speak out on the need for Catholics to seek reconciliation with Protestants and for church leaders to stop interfering in matters of purely scientific research. Now he was on a more pressing mission: to bring God's message to an island long since stripped of any vestige of faith, hope, or love.

Sam Mudd could hardly believe his good fortune. It was a Christmas present he would remember the rest of his life. Freed from his chains and "dressed in my best," although surrounded by a retinue of guards, he went down to participate in the service and visit with the churchmen. At this time he received a letter from his cousin Ann,[11] containing a crucifix, a scapular, and some other items, which had been forwarded through Father O'Hara. That evening, Bishop Verot gave "a very learned and practical lecture," following which he visited Sam in his cell and heard his confession.

Father O'Hara stayed another week, but Bishop Verot left the next day after saying Mass one more time and giving Mudd a special blessing. In summing up his views of the clerics, Mudd found Father O'Hara to be "a very pious man" and "a fine preacher." Bishop Verot, he said, was "a most saintly man, plain and unassuming as an old fiddlestick."

Still another reason for the improvement in Dr. Mudd's morale as 1865 drew to a close was an unexpected relaxation of some of the brutal punishment he had been suffering since his escape attempt three months before. Unbeknownst to him at the time, his wife had finally gotten through to President Johnson.

---

[11] Sister Joseph of the Carmelite nuns

Chapter /Ten

Help on the Home Front

In most of his letters from Fort Jefferson, Dr. Mudd complained about the living conditions and the fact that no one appeared to be doing anything to get him a pardon. What he failed to realize was that his relatives back home had almost as many problems as he did.

When the soldiers carted her husband off to jail in April 1865, Sarah tried to look brave and hopeful. The whole thing was nothing more than a big mistake, she kept telling herself. It was a nightmare that would go away the minute she pinched herself and woke up. But it didn't go away and she didn't wake up. Nor did Sam come back

like everyone said he would. Instead, he had been
moved from that dirty old firetrap near the
Capitol to a warship anchored out in the
Anacostia River and then to the Arsenal penitentiary with a bunch of people accused of murdering
the President. It was unbelievable. It was crazy.
Even worse, it was actually happening.

Not long after the soldiers arrested Sam
Mudd, another group showed up at the farm, just
in case Booth should come back unexpectedly.
When he didn't, they became irate.

In retaliation they burned the fences at the
Mudd farm, destroyed the crops, and pulled the
boards off a storehouse so that the ears of corn
spilled out onto the ground. The meathouse was
broken open and the contents stolen or thrown
away. Rings of horsemen kept people from entering or leaving except at certain times. The ser-
vants were menaced. And Sarah was searched
once by an officer who suspected that she was carrying food to Booth.

Without a man in the house to protect her,
Mrs. Mudd never knew whether or not the soldiers planned to kill her. One night was especially
bad. With the troops outside shouting threats and
insults, she put the children to bed, pulled down
the curtains, and locked the doors. Then came a

sinister knocking after midnight, and she figured the end had arrived. Happily, the mysterious visitor turned out to be her cousin Sylvester, who had sneaked through the picket lines to guard her in her time of need. Together they sat up all night, talking to maintain their courage. The next day they received the glad news that Booth had been located and the soldiers were heading back to Washington.

Still the pressure continued. One day a wagon drove up into the yard, and a lieutenant announced that they had come to take Mrs. Mudd into town for questioning. When asked if she could ride in the next day after doing some chores, the lieutenant gallantly replied that he would trust her and lumbered off in a cloud of dust.

She never found out what the Army wanted with her. The next morning she and her brother Jere took a stage into Washington, where they were met by a cavalry unit and escorted to Lafayette Baker's office. Baker saw them, said a few brief words, and told Mrs. Mudd to come back the following day. She returned but pleaded that she was worried about her small children at home. He, in turn, told her to wait until 2 P.M. and, if she hadn't heard from him by that time, she was free to go. Since he never returned, she and Jere left without ever discovering the reason for their trip.

Sarah came into town on one more occasion after Sam had been convicted. The penitentiary was noisy, and the grounds outside were bustling with activity. Carpenters hammered away at a large scaffold, where Mrs. Surratt and the three other condemned prisoners would be hanged in less than twenty-four hours. The air was tense and security was tight. When Mrs. Mudd finally received permission to join her husband, an armed escort took up positions around the room.

Under the circumstances, the visit left a lot to be desired. The pandemonium made it difficult to hear, and the roomful of soldiers destroyed all sense of privacy. Furthermore, the distraught couple understood that this might be the last time they would ever see each other.

Glancing down at a sore on her husband's ankle, Sarah asked if it had been caused by his chains, but Sam—afraid that the guards might break up their visit—said it was nothing to worry about. They then discussed family matters, neighborhood news, and how Sarah was to run the farm in Sam's absence. They assured each other of their undying love. And they silently wondered what the future might hold. At that point, visiting hours ended and Sarah rose to leave. On the way out she passed a sobbing young woman, Anna Surratt, who had just returned from her unsuccessful trip to the White House.

Later in the week, newspapers brought Sarah the sad news: Mrs. Surratt had gone to her death, and Sam was on his way to Fort Jefferson. Looking around her, Sarah almost collapsed with despair. In addition to the various reminders of Sam, she saw a wrecked farm and four tiny children. Little Andrew was six; Lillian, five; Thomas, four; and Sam II, one. Soon the older ones would be wanting to know where their father was, and how would she explain that?

On top of everything else, Sarah had to coordinate the legal work that was still being done, as well as running assorted errands to help Sam's cause. In early August she rode into town to ask Secretary of War Edwin Stanton if she could send her husband some money and clothing to make him more comfortable. Stanton, who hated Southerners and who had been the driving force behind the assassination trial, said no.

The following month she obtained an audience with the President and asked him to pardon her husband. What she didn't know was that Johnson was fighting for his own political life at the time, and that he was in danger of being impeached because of his disagreements with Stanton. As a ploy to protect himself, Johnson told Sarah that he would release Sam if the War Department agreed. So she returned to Stanton's headquarters and talked to Judge Advocate General Holt, who informed her that there was nothing he could do about the matter.

Sarah's brother Jere then contacted ex-Governor Thomas H. Ford of Ohio, a defender of the underdog and an enemy of Lafayette Baker's. Impressed with Jere's presentation, Ford approached several friends in government, including the President. With one eye on the impeachment proceedings aimed at throwing him out of office, Johnson promised that he would release Mudd as soon as he "could," adding that he didn't believe the doctor should have been jailed in the first place.

Meanwhile the lawyers filed briefs and appeals with the courts, hoping that somewhere, someone would declare the trial of civilian defendants by a military commission to be flagrantly unconstitutional. Less than a year later, they got their wish. On April 3, 1866, the Supreme Court handed down just such a ruling in the case of Lambdin P. Milligan, one of Grenfell's midwestern associates. Unfortunately, the decision didn't do Mudd any good. Stanton was out for blood, and he had no intention whatsoever of releasing the four prisoners.

Another legal maneuver occurred when the owner of Ford's Theatre hired the President's friend, Reverdy Johnson, to handle Ned Spangler's appeal and, for an additional $250, the lawyer agreed to represent Sam Mudd as well. Unfortunately, it did neither of them any good. Apparently no one seemed to remember that Reverdy Johnson was the man who had failed to get either Spangler or Dr. Mudd out of prison.

Cut off from civilization as he was in the Florida Keys, Mudd didn't know about all the steps being taken in his behalf and sometimes felt that nothing was being done at all. On the first anniversary of his arrival at Fort Jefferson, he was in a particularly bad mood. The weather was stormy, and the supply boat that day had brought no mail. Moreover, a year of prison life was beginning to wear him down.

Under the circumstances, he did something he wouldn't have dreamt of doing normally. He bawled out Sarah for everything he could think of. After criticizing the fact that she wrote only two short letters a month, never answered his questions, promised to come visit him when she knew she couldn't, and told him nothing about what was going on at home, he then analyzed her grammar and penmanship. He said he had received several letters that he could neither read nor understand because the words "were spelled backwards" and sometimes had a "whole syllable left out." He asked how he could answer her letters when he couldn't even read them.

The note did a lot to get the anger out of his system, but he began to regret it the moment he mailed it. In his next letter, and in one written several months later, he apologized for his harsh language and asked her not to be upset by what he had written. He said he had forgotten how hard she worked with the children and told her not to walk too much on a recently developed sore ankle. He warned her to be careful of prowlers after one of her neighbors had been murdered and another robbed. He told her to hire someone to help with the farm work. And he sent some gifts he had made in his spare time: large moss-cards, a cross, a wreath, a cribbage board, and a crabwood cane, plus a handful of shells he had picked up walking along the sandy beaches.

As might be expected, Sarah forgave her husband for his sudden outburst and kept after everyone she could reach to get him released from prison. In fact, it was her letter to Andrew

Johnson on December 22, 1865, which led the harassed President to order better treatment for Dr. Mudd and his fellow inmates. But Sarah knew what was bothering her husband most of all. Unlike the other three men who had been convicted with him, he was completely innocent. All he had done was set a patient's broken leg.

But at least he had his health, Sarah reasoned. Maybe Fort Jefferson wasn't so bad after all. Little did she suspect what would take place in the coming months.

Chapter / Eleven

Death Strikes the Fort

Before Mrs. Mudd's letter persuaded the President to relax the punishment her husband was suffering, the dungeon had almost killed the men imprisoned there. As Mudd described it in his letters home, the chains, the tiny cells with the tiny windows, and the lack of exercise—combined with the poor food and the stifling odor of sulfuric-hydrogen gas in the air—were enough to destroy anyone's health. Furthermore, guards yelling out the time all night long made sleep almost impossible. According to Mudd his legs and ankles were swollen, his back sore, his eyesight failing, and his sparse hair falling out. But an end to the punishment brought a return of most of his faculties.

Amazingly, his letters after that praised the health conditions in the Dry Tortugas. He talked about the warm weather and the fresh air he received while sweeping down the prison walls. On several occasions he mentioned yellow fever epidemics in places like New Orleans and Key West but said that nothing had hit Fort Jefferson yet. Their only fear, he explained, was that some ship arriving from one of the infected cities might bring the disease with it. In the meantime, he admitted that he was even getting fat on the poor food he received.

Although medical science at the time had not discovered the source of yellow fever, a few hints appear in Mudd's writings that we can now recognize. To begin with, he commented several times about the number of mosquitoes on the island and how he had to wear a flannel shirt even on the hottest days just to keep from being eaten alive. He also told Sarah that the floor of his cell filled with water in rainstorms and had to be bailed out at the rate of ten to twelve bucketloads a day. What Mudd as a doctor of the nineteenth century didn't know was that stagnant water brought mosquitoes and that mosquitoes brought yellow fever.

Without realizing it, everyone in the prison was sitting on a large powder keg, and the timer had already been set in motion. Probably the start came during the first week of June 1867, when the Gulf of Mexico was hit by three days of heavy rain, causing the fort to become saturated. This was followed two weeks later by another deluge, lasting four days and drenching Mudd's cell with more water than he could bail out. Even his bed and clothes had been soaked. Then on August 11 a third storm battered the no-longer Dry Tortugas, and within a matter of days Fort Jefferson recorded its first case of the dread "Yellow Jack."

Since Dr. Mudd had been relieved of his hospital duties in 1865 and was now working in the carpenter's shop, he apparently missed the significance of what was going on around him. Instead, his letter of August 25 expressed appreciation for the kindnesses shown him by the post surgeon, Dr. Joseph Sim Smith, and the new post commander, Major Valentine H. Stone. In exactly a month, both Smith and Stone would be dead.

On August 26, a second yellow fever victim was admitted to the hospital, and Mudd predicted the poor man wouldn't live. After that, the tiny trickle of patients became a regular flood. By September 3, there had been three more deaths, and part of the garrison had been moved to one of the neighboring islands.

Threatened as they were, the prisoners saw a faint glimmer of hope in the mounting tragedy. They thought that now the Army would have to abandon Fort Jefferson and move them elsewhere. Mudd told Sarah to pass the word along to as many people as possible so that they could start a campaign, demanding transfers in the name of humanity.

Regardless of humanity it was an act of God that Mudd was there when he was, because Dr. Smith admitted he had never seen a case of yellow fever before and soon became one of its victims. Mudd, who had learned a little about the disease while in medical school during the epidemic of 1855, took over the hospital. At the same time, Colonel Grenfell moved in and named himself head nurse. Both men worked day and night, for weeks on end, and between them undoubtedly saved dozens of lives, but Dr. Smith was not among the fortunate ones.

Joseph Sim Smith had attended Georgetown College in the class a year behind Mudd's and had joined the Union army as a surgeon in 1862. By the end of the war, he had reached the rank of brevet major and apparently planned to make a career out of the military. It was an unkind fate, however, that brought him to Fort Jefferson on July 31, 1867, along with his wife and two young children.

Of all the families on the island, few suffered more severely than did the Smiths. The parents were stricken during the first week of September, and Dr. Smith died on the seventh. Mrs. Smith recovered. Sam sympathized with all the patients in the hospital, but his heart most especially went out to Dr. Smith's son, probably because he missed his own children so much. On September 16 he wrote to Sarah:

> *Dr. Smith's child, a boy about three years old, has the fever. He is a very intelligent child, and has amused me on several occasions. I fear he will not get over it. . . . A little daughter about seven years old remains exempt, having been sent to a different portion of the fort. The little boy was very fond of me, and used to turn somersaults for me.*

A day later he added:

> *I visited my little pet to-day, and found him, to my great sorrow, almost in the agonies of death.*

And then on September 18:

> *The little son of Mrs. Smith died at 3 o'clock this morning; poor woman, she has lost her husband and son—not being here more than six weeks. A little girl only survives; she will leave by the first boat for the North.*

In his depression, Sam didn't bother telling Sarah that young Henry Smith had actually died in his arms.

Now it was time to turn from the dead to the living, and Mudd gratefully acknowledged the arrival of reinforcements in the form of Dr. D. W. Whitehurst, an elderly surgeon from Key West. Two extra hands were a big help, but Mudd felt frustrated to be merely treating symptoms rather than getting at the actual cause of the disease. If a patient was cold, you put blankets on him. If he was hot, you bathed him in cool water. And if his stomach was upset (a common condition with yellow fever), you gave him medicine to settle it down. But how do you stop the spread of an epidemic when you don't even know what is responsible for it?

Suspecting that the victims were passing the infection along to one another through a mysterious process called miasma, Mudd and Dr. Whitehurst put the patients in four different buildings on the surrounding islands. Neither they, nor

anyone else, would discover for several more
decades that the *Aedes aegypti*, or African mosquito,
was the real culprit and that it could fly from island
to island, spreading the disease as it went.
In addition to being fatal in many cases,
yellow fever was extremely painful. It usually
started with a severe headache and the pain went
down the spine until it hit the backs of the legs.
Because of these various aches, the illness was
sometimes called bone fever. And just when it
seemed to be clearing up and the patient thought
he was cured, it came back again, worse than
before. It brought with it chills, fever, and almost
unbearable thirst. In its final stages, it turned the
victim's skin yellow.

For those who didn't die, recovery was rapid,
and they were often back at work within ten days.
While in the hospital, however, patients required
almost constant attention by Grenfell, his assistant nurses, and the two doctors. Many of Sam's
letters home were written late at night, when he
said that he had to make one more round of the
wards before grabbing a quick nap.

Besides the Smith family, there were other
personal losses, such as the newly arrived lieutenant who had been nice to Mudd and who had
been the only healthy officer in the entire fort on

September 13. Eleven days later he was carried out to be buried.

A third officer noted for his sympathetic treatment of Dr. Mudd was the post commander, Major Stone. On September 21, Mrs. Stone died, and her husband left by ship the following day to get his 2-year-old son out of danger. Thanks to this prompt action, the child was saved but not the father. Major Stone had caught the disease before leaving Fort Jefferson and he died in Key West, just four days after his wife.

Sam Arnold recovered from his attack. Michael O'Laughlin didn't. The former Confederate soldier, a boyhood playmate of Booth's, died on September 23, while Dr. Mudd sat beside him, desperately applying cold rags to break the fever.

Death was sad and often wrenching, but there was no time for fancy farewells. The moment a person died—and sometimes before he died—a plain wooden box was brought alongside his bed so that the infected body could be removed from the hospital as rapidly as possible. Less than thirty minutes after one of the doctors certified that death had occurred, the burial party moved in. They placed the body in the waiting coffin, nailed the lid shut, carried their burden down to a boat, rowed nearly a mile to another island, dug a hole, lowered the coffin in, covered up the hole, and rowed back to Fort Jefferson.

Duty on the burial details was not popular. In addition to the hard work involved, there was the fear that whoever picked up the dead body or touched the blanket he was wrapped in might come down with the fever himself. Therefore, the men selected to handle the distasteful task were given liberal doses of whiskey. According to Dr. Mudd, this didn't make the work any safer or easier, but it did put the men in a better mood.

On September 24, the day after Michael O'Laughlin died, Colonel Grenfell's exhaustion caught up with him. Tired and weak from loss of sleep, the old soldier finally collapsed and had to be put in bed alongside his dying patients. Because of his age and hard work as chief nurse, he had little strength left to fight the deadly disease, and Dr. Mudd sadly decided that he wasn't going to make it. But a man who has lived through wars with Arabs, South Americans, North Americans, Indians, and Russians isn't easy to kill. Somehow or other, he lived.

Dr. Mudd, on the other hand, almost didn't. While taking care of Grenfell, Mudd came down with the splitting headache, the back pains, the chills, the fever, and was hospitalized himself.

Immediately, two volunteer nurses moved in to watch over him twenty-four hours a day, taking turns at bathing him in cool water and wrapping him in blankets. They mopped his brow when the sweat poured off and dug into his medicine chest for the drugs he had given the other patients. They slept in shifts and they ate in shifts. They even worried in shifts. And when he finally woke up, there they were: the other Lincoln conspirators, Sam Arnold and Ned Spangler, to whom Sam Mudd had become a hero.

❖ ❖ ❖

By the time Dr. Mudd had recovered enough to get up on October 14, the worst of the epidemic was over. But it had left a terrible toll. Of the approximately three hundred people at Fort Jefferson—including soldiers, civilians, and prisoners—some 270 had been struck down by yellow fever and 38 had died. For some reason Sam could never figure out, the soldiers suffered worse than the prisoners and the whites worse than the blacks. He was also amazed at the speed with which the disease swept all before it.

On the night of September 16, Company M had gone to bed healthy and congratulating itself on recording the fewest number of sick calls on the island. By midnight, its sergeant was pleading with Dr. Mudd for help, since half of the sixty men were writhing in pain and the other half didn't know what to do for them. Two days later, the other thirty men were taken ill, and an entire company of soldiers had been put out of action—some never to recover.

Among those who lived, there was a certain sense of closeness and camaraderie common to any group of people who have survived a major disaster. For their part, Arnold and Spangler felt a special tie to the man whose life they had saved.

In return, Dr. Mudd showed an amused partiality toward the uneducated carpenter who had also been a favorite of Booth's, despite his habit of drinking too much and working too little. Spangler became Mudd's cellmate during the epidemic and served the dual purpose of entertaining everyone with a steady stream of jokes and of keeping visitors away whenever the tired physician lay down to rest for a few minutes. Even the soldiers, who had originally hated the four Lincoln conspirators, found it impossible not to laugh at the shabby, unshaven prisoner with the droll sense of humor.

The greatest overall change of feeling after the epidemic, however, dealt with Dr. Mudd. As soon as he took over from Dr. Smith, he was given the run of the fort. For him there were no more

Edman (Ned) Spangler, one of Dr. Mudd's fellow prisoners at Fort Jefferson. After the two had been freed, Spangler spent his declining years at the Mudd farm.

locked cells, no more chains, and no more carrying or cleaning bricks. Now he could come and go as he pleased, and he enjoyed the heady experience of being looked up to by the enlisted men and being treated as a gentleman by the officers.

On a more concrete level, this gratitude took the form of a petition to President Johnson asking that Dr. Mudd be released from prison and returned to his family. Signed by everyone present, the document stated that Mudd's medical skills, courage, and unselfishness had saved countless lives and prevented a dangerous panic. "Many here," it concluded, "who have experienced his kind and judicious treatment, can never repay him the debt of obligation they owe him."

Based on this, Mudd justifiably thought he would soon be free. In fact, the 1936 movie *The Prisoner of Shark Island* leads viewers to believe that the petition ended Mudd's sufferings and sent him sailing home shortly thereafter to a joyful reunion with his wife and children. Unfortunately, real life didn't work that way.

When the post commander, Major Stone, left with his young child, he promised to personally present Dr. Mudd's case to General Grant once he got back to Washington. The problem was, Stone never got back to Washington. He died in Key West, and his message died with him. A month later, the petition also died a mysterious death. It just vanished in the War Department files, not to be seen again for more than one hundred years.

To make matters worse, the new commanding officer, Major George P. Andrews, hadn't suffered through the epidemic and wasn't as favorably disposed towards the prisoners as Stone had been. In addition to disposing of the petition, he threw the remaining conspirators back into their cells and ordered their chains put on once again.

Chapter / Twelve

The Colonel Vanishes

As if to compensate for the sufferings of the previous summer, Mother Nature made the winter of 1867–1868 an unusually mild one. Writing to one of his snowbound friends in Indiana, Colonel Grenfell boasted that the inhabitants of Fort Jefferson never had to blow on their fingers to keep warm and rarely even had to sleep under a blanket.

Discipline, likewise, was a mixed bag. In general, the situation was not as good as it had been immediately following the epidemic, nor as bad as it had been immediately beforehand. Despite their orders from on high, the guards

knew the heavy debt they owed to Grenfell and
Dr. Mudd, even if Major Andrews didn't. So they
made things as pleasant as they could under the
circumstances. By way of relaxation for the troops
and prisoners, someone produced a fiddle, and
Sam Mudd played at an assortment of gatherings.

Less entertaining but more encouraging was
the interest that Congress had begun to display in
the assassination case. Early in December 1867,
William H. Gleason arrived from the mainland to
interview the three conspirators about their
knowledge of the President's murder. The defendants hadn't been allowed to testify at their trial,
and Mudd was glad to be sworn in and give his
side of the story.

Arnold and Spangler, however, were not quite
as enthusiastic, especially Arnold, who was recov-
ering at the time from an almost fatal attack of
dysentery. After all, neither of them was completely innocent, and they were afraid that anything they said might be used against them in
future proceedings.

The statements were supposed to be volun-
tary, but when Arnold protested that he was too
sick to talk, he was escorted to the interview by an
armed guard. Later he found that, if he hadn't
gone, he would have been placed in solitary con-

finement until he had changed his mind. As it was, he told the congressional representative that he didn't trust him and had nothing to add to what the government already knew. Warned to think it over, he was sent back to his cell, where he and Spangler sought Dr. Mudd's advice. Mudd shrugged. How could the situation possibly be any worse than it now was? he asked. Arnold and Spangler agreed.

But the next day, when they appeared before Gleason, the men found out what he really had in mind. Congress wasn't interested in either Arnold or Spangler as such, or even the old Booth story as they knew it. What Gleason wanted was someone to lie under oath and tie President Johnson into Lincoln's assassination. If Arnold and Spangler agreed to cooperate, he said, they would be freed from Fort Jefferson and taken back to Washington as witnesses. The offer was a tempting one, and it is to the prisoners' credit that they didn't buy it. At one point in the interview, Major Andrews threatened to have Arnold shot if he didn't help Gleason, but the former Confederate soldier stood his ground. Andrews backed down when the post surgeon intervened and told them to quit harassing a sick man.

Sometime during 1867, President Johnson

had promised Sarah Mudd that he would release her husband before leaving the White House in March 1869. Now it looked as if he might be leaving considerably sooner, and not of his own free will.

On August 12, 1867, Johnson had finally gotten up enough nerve to suspend his old nemesis, Secretary of War Stanton. In response, Congress had announced its intent to remove Johnson from office through the impeachment process. The first vote, however, had supported the President 108 to 57, and Stanton's friends were getting worried. Hence Gleason's trip to Fort Jefferson. When that failed, Johnson went one step further. This time he fired Stanton outright, and the House of Representatives quickly voted eleven articles of impeachment for violating the *Tenure of Office Act*. The resulting trial in the Senate started March 5, 1868, and ended May 26, with Johnson being acquitted by one vote.

Through all this excitement, Dr. Mudd and his lawyers kept working on their case to get him freed. Colonel Grenfell, on the other hand, had given up hope in the judicial process. With his health back to normal and spring less than a month away, he decided on a more direct means of returning to England.

From the diaries, maps, and charts he left behind him, it is obvious that the colonel had been making his escape plans for more than two years. But things kept going wrong. Either the weather was bad, or a boat wasn't available, or the guards couldn't be swayed, or there was no one willing to go with him, or the epidemic had put everyone in the hospital.

Eventually, under Andrews' dictatorship, Grenfell found three other men desperate enough to risk their lives on the open seas. One, whose name was Adair, had actually made it as far as Cuba during a prior attempt but had been captured and brought back to Fort Jefferson. The second prisoner, Joseph Holroyd, slept in a mess hall on the ground floor and could help them slip out through a nearby gun opening in the wall. The third man, James Orr, was apparently taken along because he was a friend of Adair's.

Another key factor in the escape plot was Private William Noreil, of the Fifth United States Artillery. On the night in question—March 6, 1868—he would be the sentry at Wharf Number One, where the oars and rudder of a small fishing boat had been hidden. Noreil also possessed a key to the cell occupied by Grenfell and Adair. (Orr would pry loose the bricks separating his cell from a gun casement and join the others after Holroyd had let them out through the mess hall.)

In what must have seemed to the escapees like an act of God, the garrison had been reduced to a bare minimum when most of the troops had been sent to New Orleans to quell some kind of disturbance. The *real* act of God, however, would turn out to be the weather.

According to Sam Arnold, a gale had been buffeting the fort for six days. Grenfell's crew counted on the rain to keep the guards from seeing more than a short distance and the roaring of the wind to keep them from hearing anything less than a cannon shot. On the other hand, the dangers of fleeing on such a night were demonstrated when a Coast Guard cutter pulled into the Dry Tortugas harbor shortly after dark rather than take a chance on fighting the waves.

Why Private Noreil agreed to assist the four prisoners in their madcap adventure will never be known. The Army assumed he had been bribed. Arnold maintained that he had merely felt sorry for the old man.

Around midnight, Noreil slipped away from his sentry post and freed Grenfell and Adair. Together the three men joined Holroyd in swimming the choppy moat—under driving sheets of rain and continuous, whipcrack streaks of lightning—to meet Orr on the far side. When Arnold later heard that the escapees had pushed a tiny sailboat out into the huge waves pounding over the breakwaters, he couldn't believe it. If the professional Coast Guardsmen had been afraid to challenge the storm in their much bigger craft, what chance did five amateurs have in something the size of a donkey cart? The answer left little in doubt.

After the sun rose, search vessels spread out in all directions, but no debris or floating bodies marked the final resting spot of the missing men. Nor were they ever heard from again. Colonel George St. Leger Grenfell—soldier of fortune and Dr. Mudd's chief assistant in curbing the yellow fever epidemic—had died the way he had lived, fighting with a bunch of ragtag followers against an enemy bigger than all of them.

What the Lincoln conspirators thought about this escapade is not known, but they suffered for it nevertheless. Chained in their cells and guarded even more closely than before, they accepted the confinement as just another fact of life in three years of mistreatment.

Life in the prison was hard, and Major Andrews did everything he could to make it harder. Tight mail censorship, for example, meant that all letters entering or leaving the island went through the provost marshal's office, and if he didn't like what was said, he simple tore up the document and threw it away. On at least one occasion, Dr. Mudd tried to circumvent this system by smuggling out a letter with someone headed for the mainland, but he was unable to learn whether or not it had been mailed.

In August 1868, Spangler, Arnold, and Dr. Mudd paid a Key West attorney $100 each to obtain a federal court hearing, with the promise of another $100 each if they were freed. On September 9, Judge Thomas J. Boynton ruled that the previously mentioned Milligan case didn't apply in this instance, and the Key West attorney never collected his second $300.

Two months later, Mudd submitted his last official protest. He objected that the boarding erected in front of their quarters had rendered their imprisonment "more painful and odious," but he never received an answer. Instead, the ultimate occurred.

On February 13, 1869, President Johnson kept his promise to Mrs. Mudd. He wrote her a letter shortly before leaving the White House, wanting to know if she would be kind enough to stop by and pick up a copy of Sam's pardon.

Chapter / Thirteen

Freedom

The trip to Washington was a slow one, and Sarah didn't get there until sometime on the fourteenth, but the Army had been told not to wait. The day before, the following message had been transmitted:

War Department, Adjutant-General's Office
Washington, February 13, 1869

Commanding Officer
Fort Jefferson
Dry Tortugas, Florida

Sir: The Secretary of War directs that immediately on receipt of the official pardon, just issued by the President of the United States, in favor of Dr.

Samuel A. Mudd, a prisoner now confined at Dry Tortugas, you release the said prisoner from confinement and permit him to go at large where he will.

You will please report the execution of this order and the date of departure of Dr. Mudd from the Dry Tortugas.

I am, sir, very respectfully your obdt. servant,

E. D. Townsend
Assistant Adjutant-General

Mudd was a free man for nearly a month before he knew it. The message didn't reach Fort Jefferson until March 8. Three weeks later, Sam Arnold and Ned Spangler received their letters, and all three went home. But they would never be the same again.

Arnold returned to the Baltimore area, where he wrote a book and lived to the age of seventy-two, complaining bitterly that he was still the subject of much hatred for something he hadn't done.

Ned Spangler, possessed of neither job nor money, had spent most of his time in prison taking care of the man he idolized, and now he decided that Dr. Mudd couldn't get along without him. So, one bright spring morning, Mrs. Mudd came out of the house and found Ned roosting in a tree where the dogs had driven him during the night and where he had slept while waiting to be rescued. A handy carpenter, he lived with the Mudds and helped out around the farm. He also enjoyed playing games with the children, one of whom later described him as "a quiet, genial man, greatly respected by the members of our family and the people of the neighborhood." Sam gave him five acres of land, on which Ned planned to build a home, but his health had been wrecked by prison life and he survived less than two years after arriving in southern Maryland. He is now buried at St. Peter's Cemetery in the Mudd family plot, not far from the five acres he had been so proud to walk around and call his own.

Of all the returnees, probably the happiest should have been Dr. Mudd. He had a father, wife, and four children waiting for him.[12] He had a medical practice to resume and a farm that required his attention. He had a whole countryside full of friends and relatives who believed in his innocence. And he had many years of peace and happiness to look forward to. He also experienced the pride of seeing one of his sons become a doctor and a daughter enter the religious life as a nun. But even the addition of five more children couldn't compensate for the tragedies that soon struck.

---

[12] Unfortunately his mother had died December 31, 1868, less than two months before his pardon was signed.

His son Henry, born the year after Sam's return from prison, died eight months later. Sam's father followed in 1877, and his son Andrew in 1882. Added to the loss of his hero-worshipping friend Ned Spangler, these deaths took something out of the quiet doctor.

So too did the cloud that overshadowed him the rest of his life. The country may have pardoned him, but it never forgave him. Over the years, Mudd and his family would be the targets of threats and verbal abuse from a nation that made "your name is Mudd" part of its everyday language. Furthermore, the farm had fallen into disrepair during his absence, and many of his former patients had switched over to other doctors.

In 1877, Sam ran as a Democrat for the position of delegate in the Maryland State Legislature but lost in the primary to Sam Cox, Jr., whose foster father had helped hide Booth and Herold for five days after they had left the Mudd home on their way to Virginia. Two years later, some well-meaning friends tried to restore Sam's faith in himself by nominating him as the Republican candidate for a local office in Charles County, forgetting that it was the Republican party that had sent him to prison. Sam took the whole venture as a bad joke and refused to have anything to do with it.

About the only thing he really dedicated himself to—other than his family—was his medical practice. And, once again, it proved to be his undoing. On New Year's Day 1883, Dr. Mudd rode out into a cold, rainy night to visit a sick patient and developed pneumonia. Possibly because he was depressed, or possibly because there was no one around to doctor the doctor, he simply went upstairs to his bedroom and shut himself in. Nine days later he was dead at the age of 49. Today, his tombstone may be seen in a prominent place of honor at the St. Mary's Church cemetery in Bryantown, Maryland. Ironically, it was the site of his first meeting with John Wilkes Booth nineteen years before.

Epilogue

The story of Sam Mudd did not end with his death. In fact, it is better known today than it was a hundred years ago, thanks to his determined family.

Like their father before them, the Mudd children suffered countless outrages. The taunts and jeers they encountered in life soon made it clear that they had been tabbed with the mark of Cain. Nor did the situation improve much as they grew older. With each passing year, Lincoln increased in stature until he became one of America's most popular Presidents, while anyone associated with his death was doomed to go down in history as another Brutus or Benedict Arnold.

Eventually the pressure drove Sam Mudd's third oldest to seek solace elsewhere. Marrying late in life, Dr. Thomas Dyer Mudd bought an allegedly haunted house in the Anacostia section of Washington and lost his wife to illness after she had borne him four children.

Five years later he remarried, but happiness eluded him. According to one of his sons, the ghostly mansion threw a damper on life there; according to another, the place was simply too big to mold into a home. In any event, Tom's broodings became darker and darker, and the love of his first wife hounded him until his death in 1929. As far as anyone can remember, he never mentioned the assassination.

Then, in 1936, Hollywood discovered Sam Mudd. Using a biography written by his daughter Nettie, Twentieth-Century Fox filmed *The Prisoner of Shark Island*, a highly regarded classic directed by John Ford and starring Warner Baxter.

Almost immediately, Sam Mudd was converted from a villain into a great American folk figure. Ten radio and television specials poured out in the next two decades; a hospital room was dedicated to him; a grade school was named after him; and Congress established a memorial to him at Fort Jefferson. His name even cropped up on the Watergate tapes,

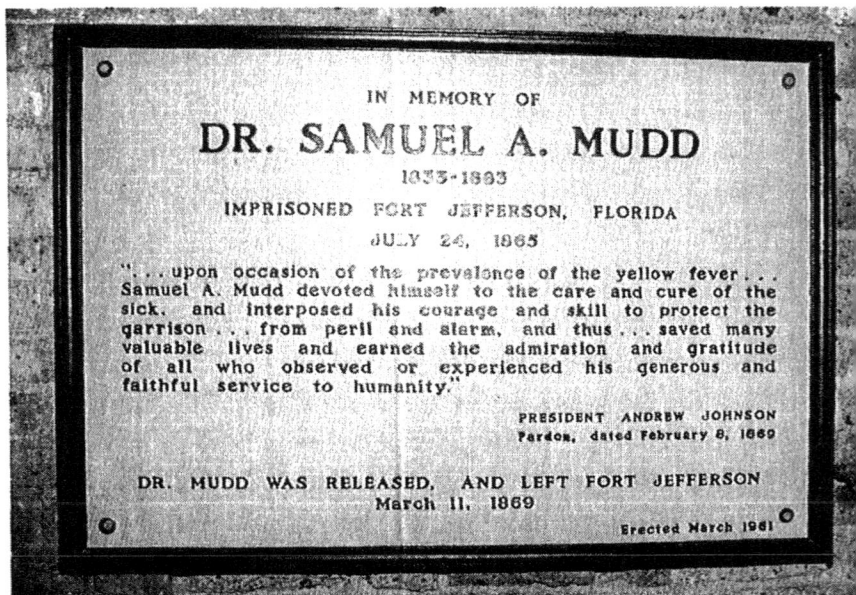

IN MEMORY OF

DR. SAMUEL A. MUDD

1833-1883

IMPRISONED FORT JEFFERSON, FLORIDA

JULY 24, 1865

"...upon occasion of the prevalence of the yellow fever... Samuel A. Mudd devoted himself to the care and cure of the sick, and interposed his courage and skill to protect the garrison... from peril and alarm, and thus... saved many valuable lives and earned the admiration and gratitude of all who observed or experienced his generous and faithful service to humanity."

PRESIDENT ANDREW JOHNSON
Pardon, dated February 8, 1869

DR. MUDD WAS RELEASED, AND LEFT FORT JEFFERSON
March 11, 1869

Erected March 1961

By order of Congress, the above plaque was erected at Fort Jefferson in 1961, honoring Dr. Mudd.

when one of President Nixon's attorneys cited the Mudd case as an example of how a person, innocent of the original crime, could later be brought to trial as an accessory after the fact.

Behind this reversal of fortune stood three people. The first was Nettie Mudd, whose collection of her father's correspondence and her mother's remembrances gave the world a firsthand account of the Sam Mudd story as seen by those who had lived it.

Continuing where Nettie left off was one of the nation's pioneering industrial surgeons, Richard Dyer Mudd, son of the moody Dr. Tom.

While still in high school, the future third-generation Dr. Mudd vowed to spend the rest of his life salvaging his grandfather's reputation, and seventy-five years later he was still at it.

Armed with a master's degree in sociology, a doctorate in history, and a doctorate in medicine when he graduated from Georgetown University and moved to Michigan, young Richard Mudd possessed all the tools necessary to carry out his campaign. In addition to writing a family genealogy, which weighs over eleven pounds, he filled his nights, weekends, and vacations touring the country, giving talks to schools and historical groups about the life of his famous ancestor. A review of his itinerary shows stops in thirty-five states, the District of Columbia, three foreign countries, and the Virgin Islands.

Worn down by this onslaught, Congress finally passed a bill in 1959 creating a monument to honor Sam Mudd at Fort Jefferson. But much still remained to be done. Both President Andrew Johnson, in 1869, and Congress, ninety years later, had simply paid tribute to Dr. Mudd's skill and courage in fighting the yellow fever epidemic. Now it was time for Phase Two. The family wanted someone in authority to say that Sam had been an innocent man, sent to prison unjustly.

Dr. Richard D. Mudd, of Saginaw, Michigan, led a campaign of more than 70 years to clear his grandfather's name.

In pursuit of this goal, Richard Mudd bombarded the White House with petitions and legal briefs, letters of support from more than three dozen congressmen and senators, and resolutions passed by the legislatures of seven states,[13] all calling for Dr. Mudd's exoneration.

Then, on July 24, 1979, the first potential break came. President Jimmy Carter wrote a two-page letter stating that, even though his staff told him he was legally unable to overturn the conviction, he hoped his opinion regarding Dr. Mudd's innocence would receive widespread circulation and

---

[13] Florida, Maryland, Massachusetts, Michigan, Nebraska, Oklahoma, and Oregon

> *restore dignity to your grandfather's name and clear the Mudd family name of any negative connotation or implied lack of honor.*

Carter's request for "widespread circulation" came true when television anchorman Roger Mudd—a distant relative of Sam's—and other members of the news corps gave the letter international coverage. But neither that nor President Ronald Reagan's letter eight years later offered anything in the way of concrete assistance.

Writing on December 8, 1987, Reagan said:

> *Believe me, I'm truly sorry I can do nothing to help you in your long crusade. In my efforts to help, I came to believe as you do that Dr. Samuel Mudd was indeed innocent of any wrongdoing.*

The Mudds had now won two moral victories but nothing of any legal consequence. At that point, the exoneration drive received an unexpected boost from an unexpected source. George McNamara, a dynamic young Philadelphia investment banker, arrived on the scene. Originally interested in convincing the United States Postal Service to issue a commemorative stamp of Dr. Mudd, he stayed on to help in what Reagan rightly called the "crusade."

For years, Roger Mudd kept television viewers posted on the latest developments in the campaign to exonerate Dr. Mudd.

Approaching his congressional contacts, espe-cially Senator Joseph R. Biden, Jr. of Delaware, McNamara prevailed upon them to ask the Secretary of the Army to reopen the Sam Mudd case and present it to a high-ranking group of civil-ian employees known as the Army Board for

Correction of Military Records (ABCMR). Chairing the board was Charles A. Chase, a great-grandnephew of former Supreme Court Chief Justice Salmon P. Chase.

When the five-man panel met shortly after 9 A.M., January 22, 1992, deep inside the Department of Defense headquarters at the Pentagon, there was a general air of excitement in the small auditorium filled with reporters and members of the Mudd family. Nine witnesses stood to be sworn in as a body, and the opening statement was made by Dr. Mudd's great-grandson, Richard J. Mudd, of Virginia.

Speaking in a crisp, quiet voice, the lead attorney painted a graphic picture of both the historical and hysterical events that had gripped Washington during the latter part of April 1865. In particular, he described Booth's flight through southern Maryland, his brief stay at the Mudd house, the search for the two fugitives, the terror inflicted on the countryside by John Boyle, and the arrest and trial of Dr. Mudd.

This was followed by a question-and-answer session between two other attorneys discussing the legality of bringing civilian defendants before an Army tribunal during peacetime. One of these lawyers was Candida Ewing Staempfli Steel, the great-great-granddaughter of Dr. Mudd's original attorney, General Thomas Ewing. The other was Colonel Jan Horbaly, an expert in the field of military justice as well as a former law clerk to Chief Justice Warren Burger of the Supreme Court. In response to Mrs. Steel's extensive probings, Colonel Horbaly explained the various aspects of martial law and stated that Dr. Mudd's trial by Army officers had been flagrantly unconstitutional.

The fourth witness was the author of this book, a retired FBI agent, who pointed out that if Lincoln had been assassinated today, the primary investigative agency would have been the FBI. The testimony presented at the trial was then discussed in detail—as set forth earlier in these pages—with the final conclusion that the government had totally failed to prove its case against Dr. Mudd for either plotting to kill the President or consciously helping Booth to escape.

Next on the docket was Dr. John K. Lattimer, a medical researcher who wrote *Kennedy and Lincoln: Medical and Ballistic Comparisons of Their Assassinations*. Dr. Lattimer not only reminded the board of a physician's obligations under the Hippocratic oath to treat those in need of medical attention but also pointed out the vital information that Dr. Mudd had given to the soldiers looking for Booth.

Laura Chappelle, a great-great-granddaughter of Dr. Mudd and an appellate attorney from the State of Michigan, testified regarding the legal limitations placed upon Dr. Mudd and General Ewing, which made it almost impossible for them to present an adequate defense. Mrs. Chappelle told the board how Mudd had been denied such constitutional rights as a trial by jury, the advice of legal counsel until the day before the trial started, and an opportunity to testify in his own defense.

Following Mrs. Chappelle were George McNamara and Thomas Boarman Mudd. A long-time teacher of American history, Mr. Mudd presented to the board a touching story of his great-grandmother, "the forgotten woman." While Sam was being arrested, tried, and held in prison, Sarah had had to deal with the travails of a father-less family, menacing Union troops, and a farm that had been all but ruined in the aftermath of the search for Booth. Finally, it was her dogged perseverance and strong spirit that had worn down a hostile bureaucracy and persuaded President Johnson to pardon her husband.

The closing speaker of the afternoon was, appropriately, the man whose lifetime dream had come down to this sudden-death hearing: Dr. Richard D. Mudd. In two more days he would celebrate his ninety-first birthday, but right now there was only one thing on his mind.

In a nervous, emotional voice, he thanked everyone who had made the hearing possible and explained what this day in court had meant to Mudds everywhere. He summarized the goal of his efforts by saying, "I hope this hearing will permit my grandfather and grandmother to rest in peace."

❖ ❖ ❖

During the latter part of Richard Mudd's crusade, the third prong of the exoneration campaign was initiated by his cousin Louise Arehart, the youngest of Sam's thirty-three grandchildren and the last to be born in the old family home.

In 1968, Mrs. Arehart asked her brother Joseph Burch Mudd, then the owner and resident, if he would be willing to sell the farmhouse and some of the surrounding acreage. When he agreed, Mrs. Arehart began negotiations with members of the Maryland Historical Trust. As a result, the building was added to the National Register of Historic Places in 1974, and both federal and state funds were made available to restore it.

Coordinating the construction work was the Committee for the Restoration of the Dr. Samuel A. Mudd House, Inc., which later evolved into the Dr. Samuel Mudd Society, Inc. Under the presidency of Mrs. Arehart, the committee found itself faced with rather extensive renovations to be made. But, by 1983, the work was completed, and a number of artifacts were added, including a couch on which Booth had rested his broken leg.

Today, the house and adjoining ten acres are open to the public on weekends from April to November, with costumed volunteers offering tours. Visitors can glimpse what the house looked like at the time of the Lincoln assassination. On special occasions there are activities such as Civil War encampments, blacksmithing demonstrations, and "Tom Sawyer Day," when the fences get whitewashed.

❖ ❖ ❖

Despite all this concerted effort, the issue of Dr. Mudd's innocence still has not been resolved.

In July 1992, all five members of the ABCMR agreed that Dr. Mudd's trial had been a gross miscarriage of justice, and the Archivist of the United States was ordered to set aside the conviction. But an acting Assistant Secretary of the Army disagreed, stating that the board was not in the business of settling historical disputes. The Mudd family immediately appealed this ruling, since the board had intervened in a number of other historic cases over the years.

Then, in 1993, three prestigious judges (including a member of the South Carolina State Supreme Court) participated in a mock trial at the University of Richmond and stated that Dr. Mudd's conviction had flagrantly violated the American Constitution. The defense team representing Dr. Mudd included F. Lee Bailey, one of the best-known attorneys in the United States.

As expected, the Army—after years of study—refused to change its mind, and the case was then taken by Attorney Steel to federal court in the District of Columbia. There, in October 1998, Judge Paul L. Friedman ruled that the Army had acted "arbitrarily and capriciously" in denying the Mudd family appeal and ordered military officials to reconsider their position.

Among those urging that the Army finally give in were Senator Carl Levin, ranking minority member of the Senate Committee on Armed Services, and Charles A. Chase, who had been chairman of the ABCMR, which had conducted the 1992 Pentagon hearing. As Chase said seven years later, "We unanimously agreed that Dr. Mudd had been improperly tried and convicted and our duty [to exonerate him] was clear."

Ignoring Friedman, Levin, and Chase, however, the Army continued to take the hard line, and as the Summer of 2000 drew to a close, the case was back in federal court. Realistically, it would appear that, regardless of whichever side wins, appeals will be filed down the road, and the case could well drag on for another five or more years.

Certainly Dr. Richard D. Mudd made it clear where he stood on this matter. As he approached his 94th birthday some five years ago, he told a Philadelphia reporter that, if the courts refused to clear his grandfather's name, "the case will be carried forward by my children, my grandchildren, my great-grandchildren, and my great-great-grandchildren."

Obviously, then, the fight is not over and won't be until the government agrees that Sam Mudd should be exonerated.

Selected Bibliography

Arnold, Samuel Bland. *Defence and Prison Experiences of a Lincoln Conspirator*. Hattiesburg, MS.: The Book Farm, 1943.

Bishop, Jim. *The Day Lincoln Was Shot*. New York: Harper & Brothers, 1955.

Borritt, Gabor S. "Lincoln, Abraham." *World Book Encyclopedia*, 1993.

Carter, Samuel, III. *The Riddle of Dr. Mudd*. New York: Putnam, 1974.

Clark, Champ, and the editors of Time-Life Books. *The Assassination—Death of the President*. Alexandria, Va.: Time-Life Books, 1987.

Cottrell, John. *Anatomy of an Assassination—The Murder of Abraham Lincoln*. New York: Funk & Wagnalls, 1966.

Davis, Kenneth C. *Don't Know Much About History*. New York: Avon, 1990.

Forrester, Izola. *This One Mad Act . . . The Unknown Story of John Wilkes Booth and His Family*. Boston: Hale, Cushman & Flint, 1937.

Grun, Bernard. *The Timetables of History*. New York: Touchstone, 1976.

Hanchett, William. *The Lincoln Murder Conspiracies*. Urbana, Ill.: University of Illinois Press, 1983.

Higdon, Hal. *The Union vs. Dr. Mudd*. Chicago: Follett Publishing, 1964.

Kunhardt, Dorothy Meserve and Philip B. *Twenty Days*. New York: Harper & Row, 1985.

Lattimer, John K. *Kennedy and Lincoln: Medical & Ballistic Comparisons of Their Assassinations*. New York: Harcourt Brace Jovanovich, 1980.

McClure, Stanley W. *Ford's Theatre: National Historic Site*. Washington, D.C.: U.S. Government Printing Office, 1984.

Mudd, Nettie. *The Life of Dr. Samuel A. Mudd*. New York: Neale Publishing, 1906.

Pitman, Benn. *The Assassination of President Lincoln and Trial of the Conspirators*. Cincinnati: Moore, Wilstach, and Baldwin, 1865.

Roscoe, Theodore. *The Web of Conspiracy*. Englewood Cliffs, NJ: Prentice-Hall, Inc., 1959.

Smith, Gene. *American Gothic: The Story of America's Legendary Theatrical Family—Junius, Edwin, and John Wilkes Booth*. New York: Simon & Schuster, 1992.

Starr, Stephen Z. *Col. Grenfell's Wars*. Baton Rouge: Louisiana State University. Press, 1971.

Surratt Society. *From War Department Files: Statements Made by the Alleged Lincoln Conspirators Under Examination 1865*. Clinton, MD: 1980.

United States National Park Service, Department of the Interior. *Fort Jefferson National Monument, Florida*. Washington, D.C.: U.S. Government Printing Office, 1984.

Ward, Geoffrey C., and Ric Burns. *The Civil War: An Illustrated History*. New York: Knopf, 1990.

Weckesser, Elden C. *His Name Was Mudd: The Life of Dr. Samuel A. Mudd, Who Treated the Fleeing John Wilkes Booth*. Jefferson, N.C.: McFarland & Co., 1991.

Weichmann, Louis. *A True History of the Assassination of Abraham Lincoln and of the Conspiracy of 1865*. New York: Knopf, 1975.

Index

www.ingramcontent.com/pod-product-compliance
Lightning Source LLC
Chambersburg PA
CBHW060355090426
42734CB00011B/2141